## Praise for *Working with SDI*

"*Working with SDI* is an outstanding resource for improving relationships. This book is guaranteed to help you deepen your knowledge of the SDI and build stronger relationships, even with the most difficult people you encounter."

— **Peter B. Stark**, speaker & consultant, Peter Barron Stark Companies, Inc.; co-author, *The Competent Leader*

"Relationships are the currency of business; knowing how to build productive and enduring relationships is a critical skill for those who seek success and fulfillment at work. *Working with SDI* adeptly demonstrates how learning about others and applying your strengths enables you to build mutually beneficial relationships. In the process, you learn a lot about your personal brand. The authors clearly state that a book about relationships is not substitute for learning in relationships, but this guide is a valuable resource that helps you understand key concepts and apply them to your daily interactions."

— **William Arruda**, CEO, Reach Personal Branding; author, *Ditch. Dare. Do! 3D Branding for Executive Success*

"As the authors suggest, this book describes different personality types based on concepts in Relationship Awareness Theory and the Strength Deployment Inventory (SDI). It does that very well and in an enjoyable and engaging manner. The approach is well crafted and articulated.

*Working with SDI* provides a valuable resource for anyone wishing to learn about themselves, develop skills in self-management and relationship management, and become more effective as a manager or team member.

Unlike many 'self-help' or personal improvement books, this one is based on credible theory and supporting research. The reader is not asked to accept suggested approaches and methodologies on faith. Instead, everything in *Working with SDI* is well explained and documented.

This clever book can be read at different levels and for different purposes. The authors recognize that their book may not be assimilated in a single con-tinuous read, but rather is intended as an ongoing resource. It works. The reader will not be disappointed!"

— **Jay Finkelman,** PhD, ABPP, vice president of academic affairs, chief academic officer, The Chicago School of Professional Psychology

"Scudder and LaCroix connect the thinking of Jung, Freud, Fromm, Rogers, and Porter, allowing users of the SDI to make sense of their own 21st century situations. Since being introduced to the SDI in the early 1990s, I have shared its valuable teachings with thousands of people in over 50 countries and have dedicated a good part of my career to uncovering the connections between the SDI and the achievement of optimal outcomes in dialogue, negotiation, and business development. I recommend this book to people wanting to understand the foundations that allow the SDI to stand above the many competing tools and inventories now available. By creating this text, the authors have proven themselves to be both the sculptors and the marble as this book will undoubtedly help thousands more people achieve the fruits of improved relationships at work, at home, and in society. Thank you."

> — **Peter Nixon**, FCPA, MSc., managing director, Potential Dialogue; author, *Dialogue Gap* and *Negotiation: Mastering Business in Asia*

"I have waited a long time for this book—without knowing that I was waiting for it. *Working with SDI* is now a key resource in my library. It's full of personally and professionally useful insights."

> — **Ginny Barnhill**, SPHR-CA, CPT, training and staff development professional, GEI Consultants, Inc.

"We judge ourselves by our internal intentions. We judge others by their external behaviors. The different perceptions may be extensive and perplexing. *Working with SDI* will help you clarify the confusion, understand your perceptions, and build more effective relationships."

> — **Elaine Biech**, president, ebb associates inc; author, *The Business of Consulting,* and editor, *The ASTD Leadership Handbook*

"In my previous company, we used the Strength Deployment Inventory (SDI) and Portrait of Personal Strengths as the centerpiece of building people skills in the Lean Sigma Black Belt workshop for over 12 years. We found that knowing yourself, having an appreciation for others' personalities, and understanding what triggers conflict were critical skills for Lean Sigma Black Belts or Improvement Advisors. Building strong, trusting relationships is one of the most important elements to enable successful improvement and get faster results. We also found success in teaching leaders and their work teams about Relationship Awareness Theory and using SDI. This book provides an in depth understanding of the SDI tool and why it works. It compliments the training and provides an easy-to-use reference for those applying Relationship Awareness Theory."

> — **Bruce Boles**, Lean Sigma Master Black Belt and Improvement Consultant

"The focus of the SDI is on the motivation that drives behavior. This book is an essential read for any person seeking to understand the SDI for themselves, or to present it to others. This book has greatly added to my own appreciation of the substance of the SDI, and its utility in helping people explore the 'why' of their lives and actions. With explanations about the theoretical connections to Freud, Jung, Fromm, Rogers, Porter, and Maccoby…this book provides us with invaluable insights that will translate into enhanced SDI facilitation. I highly recommend it for your tool kit."

> — **Dr. John L. Harrison, Sr.**, SPHR, associate professor of leadership and management

"A handy reference guide that will help you maintain productive relationships and speed through the unexpected rocky stretches that inevitably appear when people strive to achieve great things."

> — **Dawn Papaila,** MA, CPT, president and principal consultant, WLP Consultants, and director, International Society for Performance Improvement (ISPI), 2010-2012

"I have been using the full suite of SDI assessments for over ten years. They are extremely powerful team development tools—especially for teams who have defined themselves as being 'in conflict.' This new book, *Working with SDI*, offers a fresh look at principles for improving relationships at work and at home. It's a must read for seasoned facilitators and those new to the topic."

> — **Gene Mickelson**, education director, VA Midwest Health Care Network

"This is a great resource that can help anyone improve their personal and professional relationships."

> — **De'Onn Griffin**, PhD, global learning and development leader, Carlson Wagonlit Travel

"Being new to the SDI world, I found this book a fitting companion to the SDI Facilitator Certification. For me, it is a field guide, a textbook, and the next volume in an ongoing philosophical discourse on the importance of awareness. I find especially useful the 'things to avoid when approaching people while they are in Stage 1 conflict.' This indispensable wisdom is now part of my reference collection for my child protective services social work."

> — **Colette Street**, MSW, MA, professional child protective services social worker, County of Los Angeles

# WORKING

*with*

# SDI

How to Build More Effective Relationships with
the Strength Deployment Inventory

*by*

Tim Scudder & Debra LaCroix

PERSONAL
STRENGTHS
PUBLISHING

Personal Strengths Publishing, Inc.
P.O. Box 2605
Carlsbad, CA 92018 USA

www.personalstrengths.com

**Cataloging-In-Publication Data**

Scudder, Tim.
   Working with SDI: how to build more effective relationships with
the Strength Deployment Inventory / Tim Scudder, Debra LaCroix. —1st ed.
     p. cm.
  Includes index, notes, and bibliographical references.
  ISBN: 978-1-932627-17-6
1. Interpersonal Relations. 2. Psychology. 3. Employee Motivation. 4. Leadership.

Printed in the United States of America
FIRST EDITION

*"The more a personality theory can be for a person, rather than about a person, the better it will serve that person."*

— Elias H. Porter

# Contents

## PART 4 : GOING FURTHER

# How to Use This Book

This book is intended to help you improve relationships, whether they are at work, at home, with friends, or in your community. It's been said that "It's not what you know, but who you know" that matters. That might be true for networking, but for sustainable relationships, it's what you know about who you know that makes the difference.

This book is intended to help you increase your knowledge of yourself and others. With that knowledge, you can build more productive, mutually rewarding, and sustainable relationships. You can also anticipate and prevent some of the unnecessary conflict that happens all too frequently in relationships and identify conflict more quickly when it does happen, so you can do a better job of managing it and bringing it to productive resolution.

## OVERVIEW

Ideally, you are reading this book because it is part of a personal or professional development experience that has been or will be led by a facilitator or coach. No book about relationships can take the place of learning in relationships, but it can be a useful supplement. And your learning in relationships is not limited to a classroom or other structured environment. Learning in relationships happens every single day—if you let it.

This book describes different types of personalities based on concepts in Relationship Awareness Theory and the *Strength Deployment Inventory (SDI)*. It is unlikely that most people will read it straight through from cover to cover. Instead, the book is intended to provide you with a resource as you continue learning and as you continue to develop your skills in self-management and relationship management. You will find ideas about how to engage your strengths to become more productive in your relationships, and how to help others engage their strengths to become more productive.

To get the most from this book, you should know your Motivational Value System and Conflict Sequence as reported by the SDI. Ideally, you also will have considered your personal strengths and the way your strengths may sometimes get overused. The *Portrait of Personal Strengths*, and the *Portrait of Overdone Strengths* are useful in this regard.

To get started, you might want to first read the chapter "The SDI Language of Relationships." This will help you solidify your understanding of the key concepts presented in this book and how these concepts are connected to each other.

## CHECKING YOUR OWN RESULTS

Next, consider refreshing your memory about the different personality types described in Relationship Awareness Theory by reading the "SDI Results at a Glance" section. This will lead you into the section that describes each Motivational Value System (MVS) in detail. If you're like most people, you'll probably want to take a look at your own MVS first, and if your MVS dot is near the border of another MVS region on the triangle, you'll probably want to take a look there too.

You'll likely be curious about the arrowhead, which was drawn from the conflict scores of the SDI. If so, read the information about your Conflict Sequence and any other Conflict Sequences that are close to yours.

## THINKING ABOUT OTHERS

If you participated in a workshop experience, you probably know the SDI results of several other people. Take some time to read the detailed descriptions about their personality types, and some of the suggestions about how to work more effectively with them and how to prevent unnecessary conflict with them. If you want to think about people for whom you do not know their SDI results, take a look at the "SDI Results at a Glance" section, and make educated guesses based on your experiences and perceptions of them. Then read the detailed sections to see if the descriptions fit.

At this point, with information about yourself and others in mind, you may find it useful to read the "Overview of SDI" section and the introductory parts of the "Motivational Value Systems" (Part 2) and "Conflict Sequences" (Part 3) sections. Together, these sections will help you fit the concepts together and come up with ideas about how you can improve the quality of your relationships and the quality of results produced in those relationships.

## MAKE IT YOURS

 Write in this book. Fold the pages. Insert sticky notes and bookmarks. Draw stars and emoticons in the margins. Whenever you find something insightful or useful, highlight it. Make it easy to find later. If you disagree with something, cross it out. This is a book for you to use. Ideas aren't useful if you can't remember or find them. So make this book yours.

# 1 INTRODUCTION

# The SDI Language of Relationships

The use of colors makes the SDI easy to remember and use. Blue is for Altruistic-Nurturing, Red is for Assertive-Directing, and Green is for Analytic-Autonomizing. In conflict, Blue is for Accommodating, Red is for Asserting, and Green is for Analyzing. The simple language of SDI gives people a shared vocabulary for conversations about complex issues of motivation, intention, conflict, and self-worth. In addition to the colors, several other terms are part of the SDI language of relationships.[1]

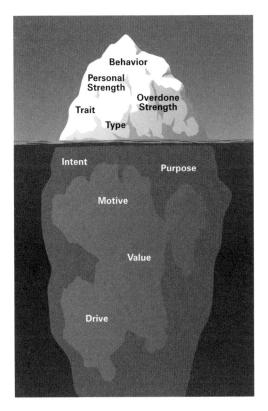

The first two sets of terms relate to the parts of personality that are external (the parts that are relatively easy to see) and internal (the parts that are more difficult to perceive). Using the iceberg as a metaphor, the external parts of personality are above the surface, while the internal parts are below the surface.

## WHAT'S ABOVE THE SURFACE?

The following terms[2] are used to describe things that people *can observe* in others:

● **Behavior**: the way a person acts or communicates.

- **Trait**: a behavior (or pattern of behaviors) that occurs frequently enough that it becomes a defining quality or characteristic of a person.

- **Type**: a category of people with similar characteristics. No individual person is a type. People in a type are more similar to others in that type than they are to people of different types, but each person in a type is still a unique individual. Consider a non-personality example: All palm trees share some defining characteristics and are easily distinguishable from other types of trees, but there are many differences in individual palm trees. People of the same personality type share some common motivations, but they may have different personal strengths.

- **Personal Strength**: a behavior or trait that affirms the self-worth of people in relationships. A behavior that affirms one person's self-worth *at the expense of another* is not a personal strength. It is classified as an overdone strength.[3]

- **Overdone Strength**: a behavior or trait that may be intended to affirm the self-worth of people in relationships but does not do so, because it is perceived negatively by one or more persons. Strengths may be overdone (or perceived as overdone) in frequency, duration, or intensity.[4] They may also be misapplied or perceived as misapplied, depending on the context.

## What's Below The Surface?

The following terms[5] are used to describe things that people *cannot* easily observe in others:

- **Drive**: an innate energizing force. People have both physical drives and psychological drives; this book's emphasis is on psychological drives.

- **Value**: a principle or standard, a belief about what is important in life. Psychological drives can be a basis for values as people develop. Sometimes, people consider their top personal strengths to be values.

- **Motive**: the underlying reason why something is done. Motives can be conscious or unconscious. The word motivation can sometimes refer to having or giving energy for a task, but this book's focus is on the purposive meaning of motive.

- **Purpose:** the conscious reason why something is chosen or done. Motives, purposes, and values can be closely aligned. The consideration of purpose can sometimes help to discover a person's motives and values.

- **Intent:** a conscious choice of behavior that is intended to create a desired outcome or effect. Motives and purposes can give rise to intentions. While intentions may sometimes sound similar to motives or purposes, intentions tend to be more closely aligned with specific outcomes.

## How Does It All Fit Together?

People are more complex than can be described by lists of traits or categories. The following terms[6] describe the parts of personality that fit together to form systems that give rise to different behaviors in different circumstances.

- **Motivational Value System** (MVS): a fairly constant set of motives and values that serve as a basis for:

  ▶ choosing and giving purpose to behavior.

  ▶ focusing attention on certain things while ignoring others.

  ▶ perceiving and judging self and others.

  Every MVS is a blend or combination of three primary motives: Blue (nurturing), Red (directive), and Green (autonomous). When SDI results are charted on the SDI triangle, the dot represents the MVS. While there are over 5,000 unique points on the SDI triangle, the triangle is divided into seven regions to distinguish seven personality types when things are going well.

- **Valued Relating Style:** a style of relating in which a person feels free to choose behavior that affirms self-worth and the intended result of the behavior affirms self-worth. A Valued Relating Style is a mix of traits, values, and personal strengths that have consistent connections with the Motivational Value System.

- **Borrowed Relating Style:** a style of relating in which a person feels free to choose behavior that does not affirm self-worth but the intended result of the behavior does. A Borrowed Relating Style is the result of a choice to temporarily set aside preferred behaviors in exchange for a desirable outcome that is expected to result from the use of non-preferred behaviors. In many cases, a borrowed behavior is a different "color" than the preferred behavior.

- **Mask Relating Style:** a style of relating in which a person does not feel free to choose behavior, but feels forced to behave in a certain way. The lack of choice may be experienced because the mask behavior helps to avoid a negative outcome, or the consequences of using a preferred behavior may be unacceptable. In many cases, a mask behavior is a different "color" than the preferred behavior. Masks may be short-term or long-term; they may be conscious or unconscious.

- **Conflict Sequence:** a series of changes in motivation during conflict that typically results in a related series of changes in behavior. There are three stages in a Conflict Sequence. These stages are characterized by a concentration of energy and a diminishing focus as follows:

  - ▶ *Stage 1:* focus on self, problem, and other
  - ▶ *Stage 2:* focus on self and problem
  - ▶ *Stage 3:* focus on self

  A conflict can be resolved or left unresolved in any stage.

  When SDI results are charted on the SDI triangle, the arrowhead represents the Conflict Sequence. While there are over 5,000 unique points on the SDI triangle, the triangle is divided into 13 regions to show 13 different personality types in conflict.

## A FEW MORE TERMS TO HELP WITH CONFLICT

Conflict can happen even in the most productive relationships. The following terms[7] describe some important concepts related to conflict, beginning with the difference between opposition and conflict.

- **Opposition**: disagreement, contrast, difference, resistance, or dissent. Opposition is not necessarily conflict, but it can grow into conflict when it gets personal. Most conflicts have elements of opposition in them. Opposition can be productively engaged when things are going well.

- **Conflict**: the experience or perception of a threat to self-worth. Conflict is generally more personal and emotional than opposition. The word conflict can also be used in everyday language to describe opposition; however, this book separates the two ideas and uses the terms as defined here.

- **Conflict Trigger**: an event, behavior, situation, or perception that threatens or has the potential to threaten a person's self-worth. People only experience conflict about things that are important to them; therefore, conflict triggers include the opportunity to learn about what matters to people. Conflict triggers also present an implied choice:

    ▶ to enter conflict based on the perceived trigger.

    ▶ to re-frame the situation so that a threat is no longer perceived.

- **Preventable Conflict**: a threat to a person's sense of self-worth that could have been prevented. Sometimes issues or disagreements are so important to someone's sense of self-worth that it is difficult to prevent conflict. However, many conflicts, especially those that develop from the perception of overdone strengths, are preventable.

- **Conflict Management**: managing the emotional experience and content of conflict and making decisions about whether to:

    ▶ attempt to resolve conflict.

    ▶ go deeper into conflict.

    ▶ leave conflict unresolved.

- **Conflict Resolution**: resolving conflict in such a way that the elements of opposition are addressed and the threats to self-worth are removed. Ideally, this also results in a stronger relationship.

- **Unresolved Conflict**: a conflict that has been avoided, without addressing the elements of opposition or removing the threats to self-worth. Unresolved conflict can be re-engaged where it was left. It can repeat and turn into habitual conflict. It can also complicate future conflicts, because new issues can get added to unresolved issues.

# Overview of the SDI

The *Strength Deployment Inventory (SDI)* is a personality assessment based on what motivates people and what brings them a sense of self-worth. When used effectively, the SDI increases self-awareness, interpersonal awareness, personal effectiveness, and interpersonal effectiveness. The journey from awareness to effectiveness, though, may be a long one, filled with opportunities to learn from successes and failures.

Even though the SDI is a personality assessment, it's also about relationships. It's based on how people are motivated in the context of their relationships with others. Working with the SDI begins with an *awareness* of self and others. This awareness can lead to greater *understanding*. Increased understanding may then lead to a greater *acceptance* or tolerance. This increased acceptance ideally leads to greater *appreciation* of self and others—and to greater *effectiveness* in relationships. New understanding empowers people to make better choices, and awareness is the foundation for understanding.

**Figure 1.1** *Levels of SDI Learning*

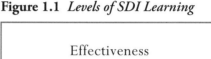

Effectiveness

Appreciation

Acceptance

Understanding

Awareness

The SDI® is the lead assessment in a suite of eight related assessments[8] that includes the following:

- **Three *self*-assessments:**
  - ▶ *Strength Deployment Inventory*®
  - ▶ *Portrait of Personal Strengths*™
  - ▶ *Portrait of Overdone Strengths*™

- **Three *feedback* assessments:**
  - ▶ *Feedback Edition*® *of the Strength Deployment Inventory*
  - ▶ *Feedback Portrait of Personal Strengths*
  - ▶ *Feedback Portrait of Overdone Strengths*

- **Two *expectations* assessments:**
  - ▶ *Expectations Edition® of the Strength Deployment Inventory*
  - ▶ *Expectations Portrait of Personal Strengths* (also available in a collaboratively sorted team version)

The feedback and expectations assessments work with the self-assessments to create rich and full pictures of relationships.

## A Brief History of the SDI

The SDI was first published in 1971. Prior to that, Elias Porter, the author of the SDI, had been working as a consultant, professor, and psychologist. Porter was a student of Carl Rogers at The Ohio State University where Rogers was an advisor for Porter's doctoral dissertation.[9] Porter joined Rogers as a peer at the University of Chicago's Counseling Center in the late 1940s, where he was part of the team that created encounter groups.[10] Porter had an experimental and measurement-oriented background[11] and was the first to measure the effectiveness of non-directive techniques used by therapists.[12] Porter's further developments of therapeutic methods were later included in Rogers' landmark book, *Client Centered Therapy*.[13]

While at Chicago, Porter began creating personality assessments based on Erich Fromm's descriptions of personality types,[14] which were an advancement of Sigmund Freud's ideas.[15] Ironically, Porter had a severe disagreement with Carl Rogers over the ethical use of personality assessments.[16] This conflict is ironic because it may have contributed to Porter's development of his own theory of personality, which states there are two conditions in which personality may be experienced and expressed differently. The first is when things are going well, and the second is when there is conflict. Rogers believed that personality assessments would lead people to accept statements about themselves that were not true.[17] He believed that test administrators would have too much power and authority, because the test administrators would choose the questions and hold the key to the answers.

Porter stated that, "the more a personality theory can be for a person, rather than about a person, the better it will serve that person."[18] He wanted to create something that would be useful for people, not a diagnostic or predictive tool. As he continued his developmental, academic, and consulting work, he created several versions of the assessment[19] incorporating features such as a primary drive for self-worth, a focus on strengths, the descriptions of the Conflict Sequences (his most original contribution to the field of psychology), and the use of colors to identify personality types. The SDI was the first personality assessment to use colors in this way.[20] As of the publication of this book, the SDI is available in over 20 languages.

## The SDI View of Personality

Many views of personality are based on behavior, or what people generally do. Relationship Awareness Theory, upon which the SDI is based, goes deeper. It holds that behavior comes from people's character structure, and that character arises from a system of personal motivations.[21] The SDI describes seven distinct ways that people are motivated when things are going well, and 13 distinct ways that people's motivations can change as they are faced with conflict.

However, the SDI does not claim that people always act the way they feel or in a manner that directly reflects their motivation. Instead, the idea is that many things come between motivation and behavior. People have different beliefs, ways of thinking, role expectations, goals, and histories. These factors and many others affect the way motivation is expressed through different behavior choices in different situations.[22]

## The SDI Arrow

The numerical results of the SDI are used to draw an arrow on the SDI triangle. For each individual, a dot represents the Motivational Value System, and an arrowhead represents the Conflict Sequence. The line that connects these two points shows that the results are from the same person. Typically, the results of several people are charted on the same triangle, which facilitates dialogue about relationships. Figure 1.2 shows a sample group triangle.

## Increasing Personal Effectiveness

Part of the purpose of working with the SDI is to become more effective in relationships. Knowing what to do in relationships requires knowing about other people and knowing about yourself. That's why most structured, SDI-based learning experiences begin with self-awareness, then move into interpersonal awareness. With that awareness, it's easier to make more informed and effective choices about behavior.

Perception comes before choice. Relationship Awareness Theory suggests that people's personalities act as filters that influence what people perceive and that

**Figure 1.2** *SDI Group Triangle*

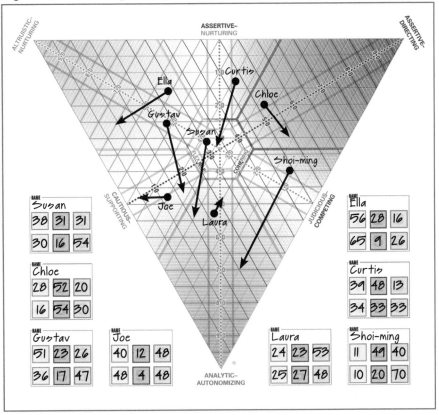

judgments or decisions based on these filtered perceptions may be limited.[23] Therefore, changing perceptions can be an effective way to be open to new ideas, to make better decisions, and to choose more effective behaviors.

The SDI gives people a common language to create meaningful dialogue[24] about intentions and motivations that might otherwise be omitted from conversations. When dialogue includes people's sense of purpose and reasons for wanting to do things, it decreases the likelihood that people will make faulty assumptions that lead to conflict and increases the likelihood of an effective interaction.

While there is no guarantee of success, the pages that follow should help you increase your awareness of yourself and others when things are going well and when there is conflict. You can use this awareness to challenge your own assumptions and perceptions, especially about why you believe other people do the things they do. You will also find some suggestions about how to borrow behavior when relating with other people.

# SDI Results at a Glance

The SDI describes personality types under two conditions: 1) when things are going well and people feel good about themselves, and 2) when things are going wrong and people experience conflict. When things are going well, three primary motivations work together as a system – the Motivational Value System (MVS). When people experience conflict, three primary motivations work in sequence – the Conflict Sequence. While these motives are given the same color names, they are expressed differently under the two conditions.

**Table 1.1** *Motivations Under Two Conditions*[25]

| Color of motivation | When things are going well | In conflict |
| --- | --- | --- |
| Blue (nurturant) | Actively seeking to help others | Efforts to preserve or restore harmony |
| Red (directive) | Actively seeking opportunities to achieve results | Efforts to prevail over another person or obstacle |
| Green (autonomizing) | Actively seeking logical orderliness and self-reliance | Efforts to conserve resources and assure independence |

## SUMMARY OF MOTIVATIONAL VALUE SYSTEMS

When the numerical results of the SDI are charted on the SDI triangle, the dot represents the Motivational Value System. Following are brief descriptions of the seven MVS types. While people of the same type are clearly different from people of other types, people of the same type will still have important differences between them. More detailed descriptions are presented in Part 2 of this book.

**Figure 1.3** *The 7 Motivational Value Systems*

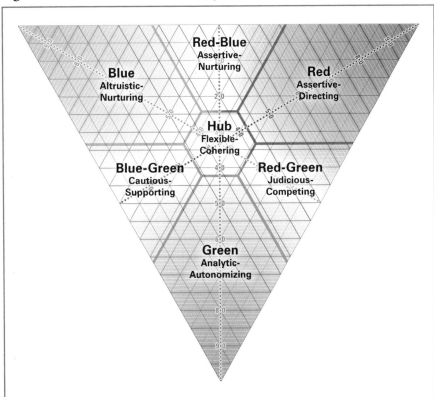

**Blue**: People who are motivated by the protection, growth, and welfare of others. They have a strong desire to help others who can genuinely benefit. (Detailed description starts on page 23)

**Red:** People who are motivated by task accomplishment and achieving results. They have a strong desire to set goals, take decisive action, and claim earned rewards. (Detailed description starts on page 31)

**Green:** People who are motivated by meaningful order and thinking things through. They have a strong desire to pursue independent interests, to be practical, and to be fair. (Detailed description starts on page 39)

**Red-Blue:** People who are motivated by the maximum growth and development of others. They have a strong desire to direct, persuade, or lead others for the benefit of others. (Detailed description starts on page 47)

**Red-Green:** People who are motivated by intelligent assertiveness and fairness in competition. They have a strong desire to develop strategy and assess risks and opportunities. (Detailed description starts on page 55)

**Blue-Green:** People who are motivated by developing self-sufficiency in self and others. They have a strong desire to analyze the needs of others and to help others help themselves. (Detailed description starts on page 63)

**Hub:** People who are motivated by flexibility and adapting to others or situations. They have a strong desire to collaborate with others and to remain open to different options and viewpoints. (Detailed description starts on page 71)

## SUMMARY OF CONFLICT SEQUENCES

When the numerical results of the SDI are charted on the SDI triangle, the arrowhead represents the Conflict Sequence. Following are brief descriptions of the 13 Conflict Sequence types. While people of the same type are clearly different from people of other types, people of the same type will still have important differences between them. More detailed descriptions are presented in Part 3 of this book.

**B-R-G:** People who want to keep peace and harmony. If that does not work, they want to take a stand for their rights. If that does not work, they may feel compelled to withdraw as a last resort. (Detailed description starts on page 87)

**Figure 1.4** *The 13 Conflict Sequences*

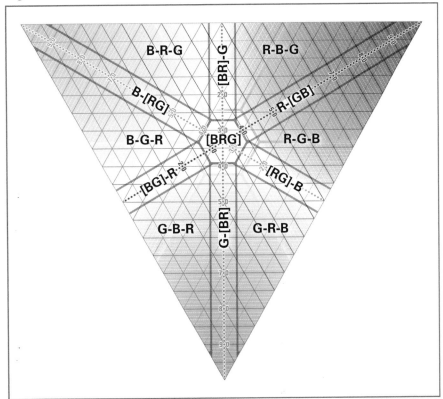

**B-G-R:** People who want to keep harmony and goodwill. If that does not work, they want to disengage and save what they can. If that does not work, they may feel compelled to fight, possibly in an explosive manner. (Detailed description starts on page 93)

**B-[RG]:** People who want to keep harmony and accommodate the opposition. If that does not work, they want to make a choice based on what's best for everyone: to rely on logic and principle or to employ assertive strategies to prevent defeat. (Detailed description starts on page 99)

**R-B-G:** People who want to challenge conflict directly. If that does not work, they want to restore or preserve harmony. If that does not work, they may feel compelled to withdraw from the situation or end the relationship. (Detailed description starts on page 105)

**R-G-B**: People who want to prevail through competition. If that does not work, they want to use logic, reason, and rules. If that does not work, they may feel compelled to surrender as a last resort. (Detailed description starts on page 111)

 **R-[BG]**: People who want to assert their rights and win. If that does not work, they want to make a choice depending on what's better in the situation: to give in with conditions or to disengage and save what they can. (Detailed description starts on page 117)

 **G-B-R**: People who want to carefully examine the situation. If that does not work, they want to defer to other people in the interest of harmony. If that does not work, they may feel compelled to fight, possibly in an explosive manner. (Detailed description starts on page 123)

 **G-R-B**: People who want to analyze the situation logically. If that does not work, they want to forcefully press for a logical resolution. If that does not work and others have more power in the situation, they may surrender. (Detailed description starts on page 129)

 **G-[BR]**: People who want to maintain order and principles. If that does not work, they want to make a choice, depending on what's more reasonable in the situation: to give in with conditions or to forcefully engage. (Detailed description starts on page 135)

 **[BR]-G**: People who want to press assertively to maintain harmony and goodwill, but they do not want to sacrifice results for harmony. If that does not work, they may decide to withdraw from the situation. (Detailed description starts on page 141)

**[RG]-B:** People who want to engage conflict quickly, but indirectly, with thoughtful strategies. If that does not work and others have more power in the situation, they may surrender. (Detailed description starts on page 147)

 **[BG]-R:** People who want to maintain peace and harmony with caution regarding the personal costs of doing so. If that does not work, they may feel compelled to fight, possibly in an explosive manner. (Detailed description starts on page 153)

 **[BRG]:** People who want to determine the most appropriate response to each situation and choose an accommodating, assertive, or analytical approach. Their approach differs according to the situation, rather than following a fixed sequence. (Detailed description starts on page 159)

## THE LENGTH OF ARROWS

The length of the line connecting the dot to the arrowhead can offer insight into the transition from the "going well" state into conflict. Generally, the longer the line is, the greater the motivational change people experience as they move from feeling good about themselves to feelings of conflict in the first stage. Since behavior arises from motivation, the change in conflict behavior tends to be more noticeable for people with long lines than for people with short lines.

**Table 1.2** *An Example of Arrow Lengths*

| Arrow | Length | MVS | 1st Stage of Conflict |
|-------|--------|-----|------------------------|
| 1 | Short | **Red** | Red |
| 2 | Medium | **Red** | Red/Green Blend |
| 3 | Long | **Red** | Green |

While the length of the line offers an easy way to think about changes between the MVS and the Conflict Sequence, it raises a different question: Is the first stage of conflict the same color as the MVS, or is it a different color?

With a short arrow (10 points or less), the dot and arrowhead are close together. The MVS and the first stage of conflict are likely to be the same color. Therefore, the behaviors arising from these two motivational states are likely to appear similar. This is why people often say that it is hard to recognize conflict in people who have a short arrow. A person with a short arrow may also experience a significant change in motivation between the MVS and the first stage of conflict, but the most noticeable change in behavior is likely to be between stages one and two, when the color of the motivation is more likely to change.

With a long arrow (25 points or more), the dot and arrowhead are far apart. The MVS and the first stage of conflict are likely to be different colors. Therefore, the behaviors arising from these two motivational states are likely to be different. This is why people often say that it is easy to recognize conflict in people who have a long arrow.

With a medium-length arrow (10 to 25 points), the MVS and the first stage of conflict may be the same color or different colors—depending on where the arrow is. Therefore, a general statement about medium-length arrows is not practical.[26]

# 2 MOTIVATIONAL VALUE SYSTEMS

# What is a Motivational Value System?

A Motivational Value System is, as its name suggests, a system of motives and values. Systems are groups of things that work together to create something that is not just greater than the sum of its parts, but different from the sum of its parts. Motives and values give purpose and meaning to activities and relationships.

**Figure 2.1** *The 7 Motivational Value Systems*

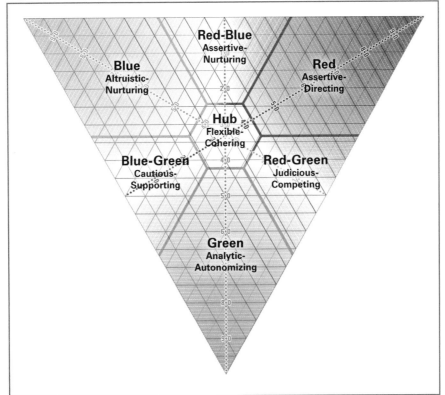

A Motivational Value System is a simple and practical way of thinking about people and personality types from the perspective of interrelated motives. The

MVS helps to explain the complex reasons that people do the things they do.

In SDI terms, a Motivational Value System is a person's unique blend of Blue, Red, and Green (nurturant, directive, and autonomizing) motivations.

All people share a desire to feel good about themselves. Different people experience these feelings in different ways, which is a part of their personality. While everyone is assumed to have all three motives, they may be present in different frequencies. The three MVS scores on the SDI, which together must equal 100 points, represent these frequencies.

These different combinations of motivations produce seven distinct personality types, as described in detail in the following pages. Three of them have a single color motive occurring most frequently; three more have two colors of motives occurring about equally; and one (the Hub) has all three colors of motives occurring about equally.

The scores from the "going well" portion of the SDI are charted as a dot on the SDI triangle to represent a person's MVS. The location of the dot suggests one of the seven Motivational Value Systems. However, when a dot is close to another MVS region (within six points[1] as illustrated in Figure 2.2), the person may identify with portions of the descriptions of more than one MVS. Unlike a typecasting exercise, the goal here is not to force a person to choose only one of the descriptions. Instead, the goal is to allow the individual flexibility to identify the most characteristic portions of each description.

**Figure 2.2** *Example of 6 Point Test/Retest*

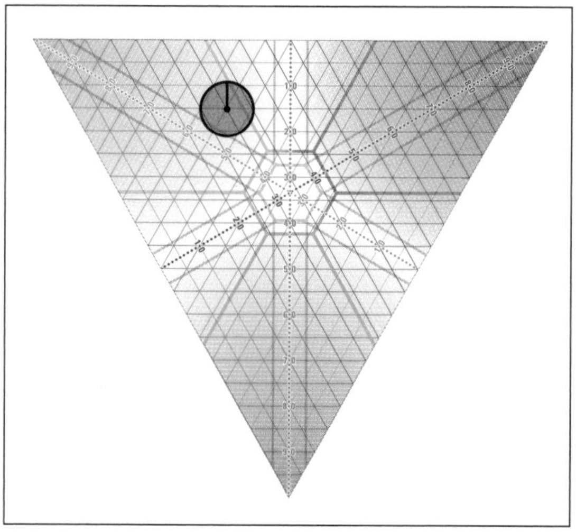

## WHAT DOES THE MVS DO?

Behavior is driven by motivation. When people feel free to choose behavior that makes them feel good about themselves, they can engage their strengths and act in ways that feel consistent with their motives. These consistent and congruent[2] experiences affirm people's senses of self-worth.

The MVS gives meaning to behavior, relationships, and situations. It acts as a filter through which life is perceived, interpreted, and understood. Filters stop some things and allow other things through. The MVS filters and influences perception; information deemed important is readily received, but information deemed irrelevant is actively or even subconsciously screened out of awareness. Differences in personal filters can help to explain why two people can have entirely different memories of a shared experience.

Behavior is a choice, and choices are limited by perceived options. The MVS can constrain or expand the range of choices people believe they have.

The MVS gives clues to sources of conflict. Because conflict is a threat to self-worth and the MVS generates feelings of self-worth, anything that restricts the fulfillment of motives can be a conflict trigger. People may experience conflict when they are cut off or restricted from acting in accordance with their own values. They may also experience conflict when acting in accordance with their values is discounted or disregarded by others.

Similarly, the MVS gives clues about how to resolve conflict. When people experience conflict, the ideal resolution allows them to feel good about themselves again. Therefore, resolving conflict requires more than dealing with people's feelings in conflict; it also requires awareness of what brings self-worth to those people. The MVS is the destination on the path back from conflict.

The MVS does not indicate skills, though people may want to develop skills in areas that interest them. The MVS is not an indicator of effectiveness. It shows why people want to do things, not how effective they are at doing them. For example, people may want to help others, but the things they do may not be helpful to others. The MVS is not a diagnosis. Just as it does not indicate skills, it does not indicate problems. While every person probably has some imperfection or development opportunity, and some of these may be common for people with similar personalities, every person is also unique.

## ARE THERE REALLY ONLY SEVEN PERSONALTY TYPES?

There are seven Motivational Value Systems.[3] People with the same MVS generally agree about why they do things; they may not necessarily agree about what to do.

Each MVS covers a region of the SDI triangle that includes many possible SDI scores. Within each region, many differences are possible for scores and also for people. The MVS scores show how frequently a person is motivated by each of the three primary motives; it indicates the relative priority these motives have. For example, everyone with a Hub MVS shares some common motivations of wanting to be flexible and bring people together. However, there may be subtle but important differences in the frequency of motivations between people on the Blue, Red, and Green sides of the Hub.[4] Within their shared flexibility, these people may place relatively different values on people, performance, and process.

The MVS is not the whole story. While the personality types described by the SDI do include everyone, they do not explain everything about everyone. The SDI's personality types are based on people's motivations—their sense of purpose and intentions. There are other, equally valid ways to describe categories of people, and these ways can usually be used as a complement to the SDI.

For example, personalities may be sorted into learning style groups.[5] Some learn best by seeing, others by hearing, and others by doing. Personalities may be sorted into groups based on levels of extraversion, conscientiousness, agreeableness, or other factors.[6] Personalities may also be sorted into groups based on mental processes, such as collecting information and making decisions.[7] When coupled with motivation, these different views of personality can offer greater self-insight and interpersonal understanding. For example, two people with a Red MVS may share similar motivations but have different styles of learning and making decisions. These differences don't contradict or negate the shared motives; they help to explain how two people express similar motives differently.

The SDI suite of assessments includes the *Portrait of Personal Strengths* and the *Portrait of Overdone Strengths*. These two self-assessments give insight into the ways that people express their Motivational Value Systems; people who have exactly the same MVS scores can behave very differently.

If the SDI shows the reasons that people do things, the *Portrait of Personal Strengths* shows the way each person goes about doing them. While any two people may have the same personality type, they may still have different strengths, or the strengths may mean different things to them. The *Portrait of Personal Strengths* is essential for people who want to create richer, more complete, and individualized pictures of their personalities.[8]

The *Portrait of Overdone Strengths* shows how people may unintentionally take their strengths too far. This awareness provides an opportunity to make better decisions and be more effective in the future.

## What next?

As you read the MVS descriptions, you may want to start with your own MVS. Make notes in this book. When you find something useful, make it easy to find again. Remember that each section is written with an MVS type in mind and that you are not a type. You are an individual. You will probably not agree with everything as presented, especially if your MVS dot is close to the border of another MVS region on the triangle.

The MVS is only half of the SDI. The Conflict Sequence is the other half. These two halves are related to each other. We experience conflict only about things that are important us. The things that triggered the conflict in the first place affect the way we experience conflict. Whatever got us into conflict provides important clues about getting us out of conflict.

So don't stop with the MVS. Get more detail about the MVS with the portraits. And understand more about your whole personality by considering your Conflict Sequence. Then do the same for other people. While the SDI is about you, it has the most value when you consider yourself in the context of your relationships.

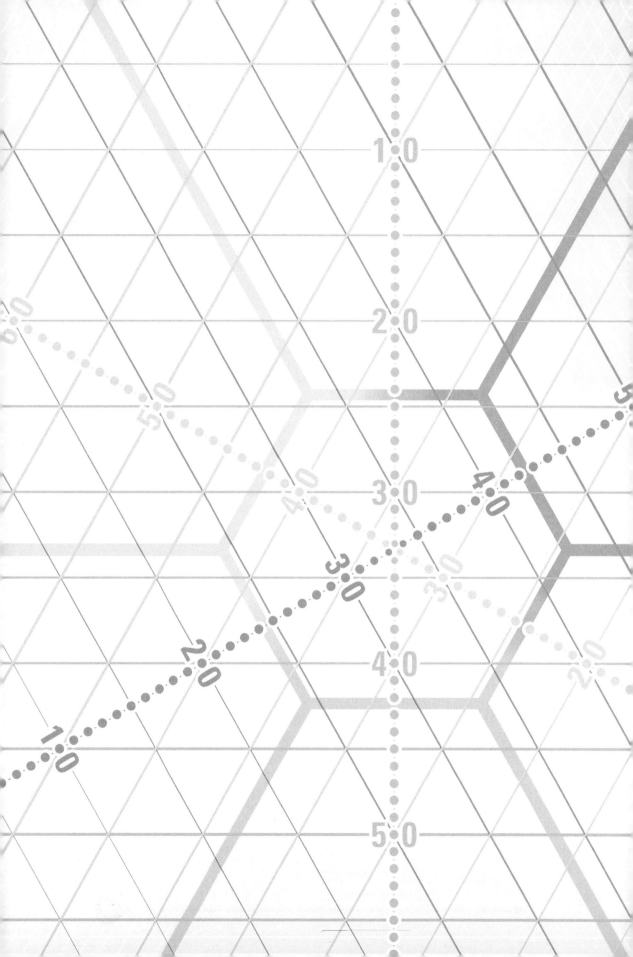

# The Blue MVS
## ALTRUISTIC-NURTURING

**Al·tru·is·tic**—unselfish concern for the welfare of others
**Nur·tur·ing**—protecting, supporting, and encouraging others

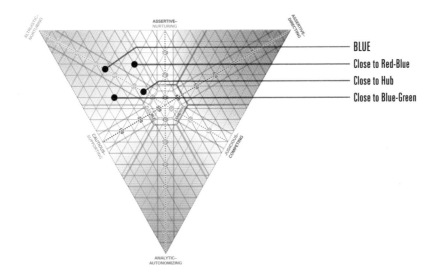

The dot on the SDI triangle represents an individual's Motivational Value System (MVS). Each person's MVS is a combination of three primary motives working together in a unique way, showing the frequency with which people are motivated by concerns typical of each motive. This descriptive text is written with an MVS dot located centrally in the Blue MVS region in mind.

Individuals with MVS dots in the Blue MVS region close to the borders (within six points) of other MVS regions may differ slightly from this description. They will likely find that the descriptions of the neighboring region(s) also influence their understanding of themselves and the way they are perceived by others.

## BLUE MOTIVES AND VALUES

The motivation of people with an Altruistic-Nurturing Motivational Value System (hereafter referred to as Blues) is to achieve feelings of self-worth by being genuinely helpful to others, with little or no concern for what they receive in return.

Blues tend to find satisfaction in life by helping others in ways that enhance their happiness and genuinely meet their needs. Blues understand the productivity behind expressing concern for the welfare of others. Blues understand and value the forgiveness of others, placing their faith in others, and offering others the benefit of the doubt. Blues believe that giving others praise and rewards creates happiness and gratefulness in the hearts and minds of those who receive the praise and rewards. Blues value the power of helping people grow.

Blues' sense of personal integrity comes from meeting the opportunities life affords to provide help to others, and the real reward for Blues is the evidence that the help was received and valued. For Blues, the effort and intent to help are most important. Blues tend to discount any thanks for these helping efforts, believing that the true reward is in the act of helping. Blues value recognition but tend to believe that any external reward for their efforts will be offered without having to ask for it.

For Blues, the act of helping is not always enough. The greatest enjoyment in the act of helping comes from seeing the other person's benefit. For Blues to experience maximum feelings of self-worth, the help must be accepted, valued, and appreciated.

## BLUE BEHAVIORS

The group of behavioral traits that Blues most frequently use is called the Altruistic-Nurturing Valued Relating Style (VRS). Blues tend to:

- Be open and responsive to the needs of others.

- Seek ways to bring help to others, trying to make life easier for others.

- Defend the rights of others with courage and conviction, sometimes without claiming their own rights in the process.

- Be idealistic and admire the accomplishments of others, often playing down their own personal achievements out of a desire to remain modest.

- Be humble, rarely asking for recognition, simultaneously putting great trust in others.

- Respond when asked for help.

- Believe that conscientious involvement will demonstrate individual worth—*and* inspire reward without request.

- Ensure that others reach their potential and are fully valued.

- Try never to be a burden to others, preferring to give help, rather than receive it.

Blue strengths confirm the self-worth of both people in a relationship. When Blue strengths are overdone, they may threaten the self-worth of Blues or the other people who perceive these strengths as overdone. Table 2.1 illustrates two examples.

**Table 2.1** *Examples of Blue Overdone Strengths*

| Productive Strength | Effect of Overdone Strength |
|---|---|
| When Blues help others in ways that genuinely benefit others, Blues and others are affirmed. | When Blues help people who do not need or want help, the help may be seen as smothering or a violation of personal space. |
| When Blues trust others who are worthy of and value that trust, the relationship is enhanced. | When Blues trust too much or trust inappropriately, they may be taken advantage of or perceived as gullible. |

## HOW BLUES ENTER CONFLICT

Blues tend to go into conflict about things that negatively affect the welfare of other people or things that restrict or discount their ability to bring help and support to others. They have difficulty with people who are overly competitive and take advantage of others. Awareness of the potential causes of conflict can help Blues to manage their own reactions to conflict triggers and can help others to adjust their behavior in an attempt to prevent conflict.

Blues may experience conflict when they perceive any of the following conflict triggers:

- Others won't accept help.

- Others change loyalties "for the moment."

- Other people are taken advantage of.

- People are selfish or unconcerned about others.

- Others are insincere about helping.

- Competition results in people being hurt.

- Behavior appears rude or unkind.

- Display of emotion is disregarded, ignored, or punished.

- Relationships are not regularly maintained.

- Issues are personalized.

When in conflict, Blues want to defend their values, so they can get back to relating to others productively. The ways they defend their MVS in an effort to return to feeling good about themselves will vary, depending on their Conflict Sequence.

## Productive Results of Conflict for Blues

When in conflict, regardless of their individual Conflict Sequences, Blues share a desire to return to feelings of self-worth and activities that support others. They are more likely to resolve conflict when they see the potential for some of these outcomes:

- Restored, renewed, or improved relationships.

- A peaceful and harmonious environment.

- Increased understanding between people.

- They will be included, needed, and appreciated.

- Greater interpersonal commitment and participation.

## How Blues Can Borrow Behavior for Increased Effectiveness

Blues' preferred approach to situations and other people may not always result in outcomes that are valuable to Blues or to others. Sometimes, nurturing strengths may not fit the situation, or they may be perceived as overdone, possibly triggering conflict in others. Borrowing behavior is most effective when considering the MVS of others, and advice about how to approach people with different Motivational Value Systems can be found in the other MVS sections of this book.

Blues may bear the burden of guilt. They want to help others, believe they can help others, and feel most rewarded when they do. When the help they offer is accepted but their efforts do not make things better for others, Blues may feel guilty that they could not find a way to make a difference for that person. They may put others' needs above their own. Blues' desire to help may make it difficult to refuse when others ask for help. Even when it is in Blues' best interest not to offer help or to refuse to help when asked, failing to be of help may result in an equally strong sense of guilt.

Blues may sometimes relate more effectively with others by borrowing non-preferred behavior such as:

- Firmly saying "no" in situations where they don't have the capacity to help.

- Clearly stating individual desires and expectations.

- Being objective and analytical in the judgment of others.

- Clarifying the urgency and priority of tasks before committing to help.

- Confidently sharing thoughts, feelings, and ideas with others.

- Accepting compliments without making dismissive remarks.

## The Blue Style of Personal Leadership and Influence

When leading others, Blues tend to focus on the needs of the people they lead, believing that people who feel supported, trusted, and cared for will be more productive. Blues view the purpose of leadership as helping others to grow and develop in their work. The Blue style of leadership is supportive and enabling, ensuring that the people they lead have the tools, resources, and knowledge necessary to succeed and to maximize their potential. Blue leadership will be characterized by:

- Efforts to maintain harmony, goodwill, and a friendly culture.

- Keeping channels of communication open, so people can build and maintain fulfilling working relationships.

- Protecting the people they lead.

- Placing their faith in the people they lead.

# Working with Blues

## INFLUENCING BLUES

The key to influencing Blues is to create or communicate conditions that are intrinsically rewarding to them. The more that what you want them to do is clearly linked to the protection, growth, or welfare of others, the more willing Blues will generally be to engage their strengths in those activities.

Blues will tend to feel more motivated in open, friendly, and socially supportive environments. They are likely to follow people who are strong, know exactly what they want to do, and work hard to include Blues in their activities.

To influence Blues, engage them in a conversation about how a desired action will:

- Benefit another person who is in need.

- Make life easier for others.

- Help others reach their potential.

- Ensure that others are valued and recognized.

## HOW TO APPROACH BLUES

- Be open, honest, one-to-one, personal, sincere, trusting, and inclusive.

- Genuinely express feelings or concerns.

- Show regard for people and appreciation for others.

- Link benefits to their effect on others.

- Listen fully and attentively, ask for their ideas, reactions, and feelings.

## THINGS TO AVOID WHEN APPROACHING BLUES

- Open or public competition, hostility, confrontation, negativity, or arrogance.

- Being aloof or distant, or appearing disinterested.

- Dismissing or devaluing their helpfulness.

- Appearing to take advantage of people.

- Assuming that silence or tentative responses equate to agreement or acceptance.

## PREVENTING CONFLICT WITH BLUES

Much conflict with Blues can be prevented by acting or communicating in ways that recognize and respect the Blue MVS and that do not introduce conflict triggers. Proactive conflict prevention strategies can be employed to reduce the chance that the self-worth of Blues will be threatened.

- Be sincere, genuine, and authentic.

- Allow time to discuss the feelings and emotional aspects of the issue or situation.

- Affirm the relationship before addressing the issue.

- Verbally acknowledge the potential threat to self-worth.

- Do not appear to patronize Blues or diminish the importance of their emotions.

- Consider the impact on other people involved.

- Check in regularly, not just when there is a specific need.

## Rewarding and Recognizing Blues

Blues like to feel that they are needed and appreciated and that the help they provided was genuinely useful to another person and made a difference. Blues may be uncomfortable asking for or accepting rewards; they generally prefer that rewards and praise be given personally, in private settings or small groups.

The best compliments are specific about the help provided and the benefits experienced. Some compliments for Blues might include:

- "Thank you. I couldn't have done it without your help."

- "Your support made my life easier."

- "You really did your job well, and everyone benefitted from your efforts."

- "You made our customers happy by sensing their needs and serving them beyond anyone's expectations."

# The Red MVS

## ASSERTIVE-DIRECTING

**As·ser·tive**—confidently self-assured and forceful
**Di·rec·ting**—giving authoritative instruction or guidance

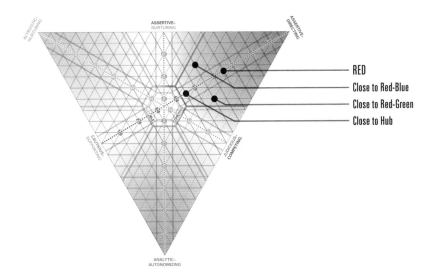

The dot on the SDI triangle represents an individual's Motivational Value System (MVS). Each person's MVS is a combination of three primary motives working together in a unique way, showing the frequency with which people are motivated by concerns typical of each motive. This descriptive text is written with an MVS dot located centrally in the Red MVS region in mind.

Individuals with MVS dots in the Red MVS region close to the borders (within six points) of other MVS regions may differ slightly from this description. They will likely find that the descriptions of the neighboring region(s) also influence their understanding of themselves and the way they are perceived by others.

## RED MOTIVES AND VALUES

The motivation of people with an Assertive-Directing Motivational Value System (hereafter referred to as Reds) is to achieve feelings of self-worth by being a successful, winning leader of others and by providing the direction needed to achieve results.

Reds tend to find satisfaction in life by being an achiever in the face of competition. They understand that in order to achieve, they must be clear about their goals and capable of giving the direction required to achieve those goals. Reds value the exercise of power and control, the setting of high performance standards, and decisive action. Reds tend to believe that the bigger the game, the greater the need to rally support to achieve success. Reds value the power of directing others productively.

Reds' sense of personal integrity comes from succeeding in a world where opportunities are constantly being discovered and where challenges are revealed so they can be overcome. For Reds, a missed opportunity equals failure. Reds want to rise to positions of ever-increasing authority, thereby creating platforms for ever-widening spheres of influence, direction, and responsibility.

For Reds, there is a desire to accomplish things and direct others—but not at the expense of others. Reds believe that competition is the "name of the game" and that winning—both the goals that they seek and the loyalty of others—is the real measure of success.

## RED BEHAVIORS

The group of behavioral traits that Reds most frequently use is called the Assertive-Directing Valued Relating Style (VRS). Reds tend to:

- Compete for authority, responsibility, and positions of leadership.

- Exert power and control to achieve results.

- Challenge the opposition, actively engaging to overcome resistance.

- Exercise persuasion, using arguments to convince and direct.

- Set goals and deadlines, allocate tasks, and monitor progress.

- Seek out opportunities that others miss.

- Take quick action, seeking immediate results.

- Claim the right to earned rewards when the results are delivered.

- Expect recognition if they've steered things to a successful conclusion.

- Accept risk taking as necessary and desirable.

Red strengths confirm the self-worth of both people in a relationship. When Red strengths are overdone, they may threaten the self-worth of Reds or other people who perceive these strengths as overdone. Table 2.2 illustrates two examples.

**Table 2.2** *Examples of Red Overdone Strengths*

| Productive Strength | Effect of Overdone Strength |
|---|---|
| When Reds speak or act directly in order to get to the bottom line, results in the relationship can be achieved more quickly. | When Reds are overly direct, they may be viewed as tactless or abrasive, which can generate resistance to action and hard feelings in the relationship. |
| When Reds are confident in their beliefs and capabilities, it can raise the confidence of others and encourage them to follow. | When Reds are overly confident, they may attempt to do more than is realistic, and they may be viewed as arrogant. |

## How Reds Enter Conflict

Reds tend to go into conflict about things that block their ability to get things done, to provide leadership, to achieve goals, and to take necessary risks. They have difficulty with people who don't stand up for themselves or withhold their opinions or ideas. Awareness of the potential causes of conflict can help Reds manage their own reactions to conflict triggers and can help others adjust their behaviors in an attempt to prevent conflict.

Reds may experience conflict when they perceive any of the following conflict triggers:

- Others do not view them as strong, ambitious people, deserving of the opportunity to provide leadership and direction.

- Others do not clearly understand the productivity behind the exercise of power and control.

- Other people view Reds' love of competition as unhealthy rivalry.

- People appear gullible, indecisive, or incapable of action.

- Others lose out because they are unwilling to stand up for themselves.

- Others keep a shell of reserve around themselves that Reds cannot penetrate.

- Behaviors directed at making everyone winners are viewed as unfeeling and/or dictatorial.

- The desire to get an immediate outcome is viewed as irrational and uncaring.

- Relationships are clouded with emotions that confuse issues and make the right choice of action difficult.

- Pursuit of the desired goal is lost through unnecessary, time-consuming collaboration or emotional considerations.

When in conflict, Reds want to defend their values, so they can get back to relating to others productively. The ways they defend their MVS in an effort to return to feeling good about themselves will vary, depending on their Conflict Sequences.

## PRODUCTIVE RESULTS OF CONFLICT FOR REDS

When in conflict, regardless of their individual different Conflict Sequences, Reds share a desire to return to feelings of self-worth and activities that lead to results. They are more likely to resolve conflict when they see the potential for some of these outcomes:

- Renewed focus on task accomplishment with a clarified direction.

- New opportunities that are innovative and creative.

- Increased energy that allows a robust exchange of ideas.

- Renewed effort for personal and team advancement.

- Willingness on the part of others to take a chance.

## How Reds Can Borrow Behavior for Increased Effectiveness

Reds' preferred approaches to situations and other people may not always result in outcomes that are valuable to Reds or to others. Assertive strengths may not fit certain situations, or they may be perceived as overdone, possibly triggering conflict in others. Borrowing behavior is most effective when considering the MVS of others, and advice about how to approach people with different Motivational Value Systems can be found in the other MVS sections of this book.

Reds may bear the burden of pride. Reds like to be the best at what they do, but no person can be the best at everything. In classic literature, the tragic flaw of *hubris* or pride makes every hero fail. When Reds are so proud they fail to assess their weaknesses adequately, they risk failure. Pride may keep Reds from hearing an opposite argument that will achieve better results or seeing the flaws in their own plans.

Reds may sometimes relate more effectively with others by borrowing non-preferred behavior, such as:

- Regulating their natural energy around issues that are important to them, acknowledging that their passion may sometimes intimidate others.

- Attending to relationships on a daily basis—not just when something is needed.

- Slowing down and thinking things through before attempting to persuade others of their position.

- Being more considerate of other people's feelings and wishes.

- Soliciting input from others, even when the right course of action seems obvious.

- Being more tolerant of people who have difficulty standing up for themselves.

## The Red Style of Personal Leadership and Influence

When leading others, Reds tend to focus on the vision, goal, or other results, believing that competition strengthens everyone involved. Reds view the purpose of leadership as setting goals and targets, defining success, and inspiring people to take on challenges. The Red style of leadership is by direction and example, initiating ambitious tasks and projects and expecting others to do the same. Red leadership will be characterized by:

- Striving for results quickly and efficiently.

- Providing rewards for innovation and performance.

- Being generous and responsive to those who are loyal and committed.

- Being willing to take risks and absorb small defeats in pursuit of long-term gains.

# Working with Reds

## Influencing Reds

The key to influencing Reds is to create or communicate conditions that are intrinsically rewarding to them. The more that what you want them to do is clearly linked to accomplishment and the direction of people and resources toward results, the more willing Reds will generally be to engage their strengths in those activities.

Reds will tend to feel more motivated in challenging, fast-moving, and opportunity-rich environments. They are likely to follow people who are generous and responsive and who want to include Reds in their success.

To influence Reds, engage them in a conversation about how a desired action will:

- Allow them to compete fairly and be rewarded for winning.

- Quickly seize an opportunity.

- Provide opportunities to lead and direct others productively.

- Engage them in a challenging venture.

# How to Approach Reds

- Be clear, direct, positive, challenging, and brief.

- Start with a goal or result, and get to the point quickly.

- Identify opportunities, and show confidence.

- Have clear time frames, end results, benefits, and relevant facts.

- Hear them out fully.

# Things to Avoid when Approaching Reds

- Interrupting, indecisiveness, giving in too quickly.

- Wasting time, not getting to the point.

- Focusing overly on social matters, details, or emotions.

- Taking undeserved credit or denying appropriate credit to them.

- Withholding information that could affect goals or task accomplishment.

# Preventing Conflict with Reds

Much conflict with Reds can be prevented by acting or communicating in ways that recognize and respect Reds' MVS and that do not introduce conflict triggers. Proactive conflict prevention strategies can be employed to reduce the chance that the self-worth of Reds will be threatened.

- Deliver important and appropriate data directly, using a point-by-point approach.

- Demonstrate an understanding of the issue's importance, and respond with an appropriate sense of urgency.

- Stand and engage with passion and energy.

- When expressing an opinion or idea, get to the point quickly.

- Deliver your ideas with confidence, as a subdued approach may be perceived as weakness or uncertainty.

- Match the Red intensity whenever possible, indicating a clear understanding of the urgency of the issue.

- Use phrases like "This is priority number one," "We need a solution now," and "What do you want me to do?"

- Focus on resolving the issue and on taking action.

- Intensify language and word choices.

- De-personalize the issue by keeping the interaction free from unnecessary emotions.

## REWARDING AND RECOGNIZING REDS

Reds like to be recognized and respected for their ability to get things done and told that their accomplishments made a significant difference in the organizational "big picture." Reds will generally claim earned rewards and will compete vigorously for the right to do so.

The best compliments are specific about the effectiveness of the direction provided and to the success of the outcomes. Some compliments for Reds might include:

- "That project would never have happened without your focus, passion, and ability to get things done."

- "Your direction and extra push made it possible for me to achieve my goals."

- "You have set a new standard that others will have to measure up to."

- "You have achieved the best results possible for this company—and for your customers."

# The Green MVS

## ANALYTIC-AUTONOMIZING

**An·a·lyt·ic**—methodical examination of structures or information
**Au·ton·o·mi·zing**—maintaining objective independence, self-governing

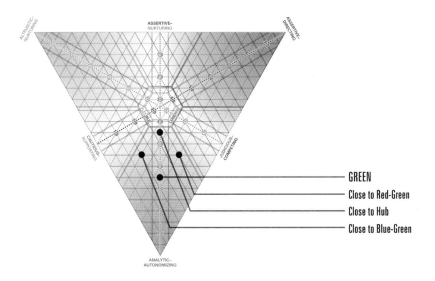

The dot on the SDI triangle represents an individual's Motivational Value System (MVS). Each person's MVS is a combination of three primary motives working together in a unique way, showing the frequency with which people are motivated by concerns typical of each motive. This descriptive text is written with an MVS dot located centrally in the Green MVS region in mind.

Individuals with MVS dots in the Green MVS region close to the borders (within six points) of other MVS regions may differ slightly from this description. They will likely find that the descriptions of the neighboring region(s) also influence their understanding of themselves and the way they are perceived by others.

## Green Motives and Values

The motivation of people with an Analytic-Autonomizing Motivational Value System (hereafter referred to as Greens) is to achieve feelings of self-worth by creating self-direction and autonomy through logical analysis and thoughtful planning.

Greens tend to find satisfaction in life through independent discovery, interpreting and explaining things based on analysis. They value the pursuit of excellence and the principled application of policies, procedures, and services. Greens understand and value the productivity behind exercising foresight, planning carefully, and attaining certainty before commitment. Greens tend to believe in the full, careful consideration of any potential action. Greens value the power of shaping order out of chaos.

Greens' sense of personal integrity comes from establishing and maintaining a sense of order, objectivity, and independence. For Greens, the real measure of success is achieving control over their own lives and emotions. Greens believe in fairness over feelings and in principles over power. Greens tend to feel a sense of self-worth when others respect them for their logic and fairness and when their right to privacy is valued and honored. Greens tend to view the preservation of resources as a means to ensure self-dependence.

For Greens, life is often about thinking things through and creating structure in whatever they do. Greens tend to want systems that minimize risks by always planning ahead. Greens prefer to rely on the use of logic, facts, and rationale, carefully weighing alternatives to ensure predictability and order.

## Green Behaviors

The group of behavioral traits that Greens most frequently use is called the Analytic-Autonomizing Valued Relating Style (VRS). Greens tend to:

- Be objective and logical, practically thinking things through before taking action.

- Be cautious and thorough, documenting details to ensure accuracy.

- Weigh alternatives, seeking solutions that are practical and fair.

- Give careful consideration to *all* costs of any plan or action.

- Maintain their self-dependence, working alone when possible.

- Create meaningful order from chaos, building systems to maintain ongoing effectiveness.

- Plan carefully, double-checking facts and preparing alternative and/or "fall back" plans.

- Approach life seriously, providing thoughtful consideration of all aspects of a situation.

- Manage their emotions, diminishing the impact of feelings on outcomes and relying on logical interaction as the primary communication style.

- Act with resolution and perseverance to implement a carefully considered, logically developed plan.

Green strengths confirm the self-worth of both people in a relationship. When Green strengths are overdone, they may threaten the self-worth of Greens or other people who perceive these strengths as overdone. Table 2.3 illustrates two examples:

**Table 2.3** *Examples of Green Overdone Strengths*

| Productive Strength | Effect of Overdone Strength |
| --- | --- |
| When Greens analyze situations in ways that enable more effective decisions, everyone involved can benefit. | When Greens over-analyze situations, they may be slow to decide; in response, others may make decisions without Greens' input. |
| When Greens are cautious, they identify risks and thereby enable everyone to avoid negative outcomes. | When Greens are overly cautious, they may become suspicious and disregard the input of other people. |

## How Greens Enter Conflict

Greens tend to go into conflict about things that restrict or limit their self-reliance, things that are disorderly, chaotic, irrational, or things that seem to be the result of biased or emotional decision making. They have difficulty with people who don't take things seriously or violate rules or principles.

Awareness of the potential causes of conflict can help Greens to manage their own reactions to conflict triggers and can help others adjust their behavior in an attempt to prevent conflict.

Greens may experience conflict when they perceive any of the following conflict triggers:

- Others force them to rush decisions and to make plans without time for the consideration of details.

- Those around them continually minimize the need for organized plans that are based on logic and careful analysis.

- Others are using broad, unsubstantiated statements as justification for their choices.

- The opposition or conflict is based in emotion.

- They are feeling pressured to accept the opinions of others, forcing unjustifiable compliance.

- They are required to jump to conclusions, making guesses or estimates without adequate time or information.

- Others imply that they are *not* fair and principled—just fearful.

- The people around them are overly helpful, unaware that the desire to help can be perceived as an invasion of personal rights.

- They are forced to do things someone else's way without adequate explanation.

- They think that others do not take things seriously, lose focus, or trivialize the importance of a calm, orderly world in which to live and work.

When in conflict, Greens want to defend their values, so they can get back to relating to others productively. The way they defend their MVS in an effort to return to feeling good about themselves will vary, depending on their Conflict Sequence.

## PRODUCTIVE RESULTS OF CONFLICT FOR GREENS

When in conflict, regardless of their individual different Conflict Sequences, Greens share a desire to return to feelings of self-worth and to activities that are logical and orderly. They are more likely to resolve conflict when they see the potential for some of these outcomes:

- Re-establishing meaningful order, which eliminates the irrational chaos.

- Re-focusing on tasks because predictable systems are working again.

- Creating more effective relationships because expectations are clear.

- Feeling a sense of independence and efficiency when all of the pieces are working together properly.

- Creating greater interpersonal commitment and participation in an improved and clarified plan.

## How Greens Can Borrow Behavior for Increased Effectiveness

Greens' preferred approach to situations and other people may not always result in outcomes that are valuable to Greens or to others. Analytical strengths may not fit certain situations, or they may be perceived as overdone, possibly triggering conflict in others. Borrowing behavior is most effective when considering the MVS of others, and advice about how to approach people with different Motivational Value Systems can be found in the other MVS sections of this book.

Greens may bear the burden of certainty. Grounded in facts, systems, and logic, Greens approach the world in a thoughtful way. Because they have thought things through before they present their ideas, they tend to be certain of their correctness, and they have the facts to support that claim. Yet, the selection of data is a subjective process. The hard truth for Greens is that no one, no matter how analytical and rational they are, can be right all of the time.

Greens may sometimes relate more effectively with others by borrowing non-preferred behavior, such as:

- Being open to uncertainty and ambiguity.

- Expressing feelings and reactions so that others will know what they are thinking.

- Accepting help from others when it could be useful.

- Ranking the urgency and importance of completion of some tasks over having all the information desired.

- Moving forward quickly and viewing activity as an experiment with an inherent learning opportunity.

- Considering emotions as additional data, becoming more familiar with what they mean to others.

## THE GREEN STYLE OF PERSONAL LEADERSHIP AND INFLUENCE

When leading others, Greens tend to focus on planning that requires logical analysis and rational consistency, believing that great systems will produce great results. Greens view the purpose of leadership as the creation of systems and structures that ensure predictable activity and use unplanned events as opportunities to improve the system. The Green leadership style is principle-centered and process-based, methodically managing people and situations. Their leadership will be characterized by:

- Establishing policies and procedures that govern organizational and individual activity.

- Developing contingency plans to reduce risk.

- Requiring individual self-reliance and rational interactions.

- Conservative use of resources with an emphasis on sustainability.

# Working with Greens

## INFLUENCING GREENS

The key to influencing Greens is to create or communicate conditions that are intrinsically rewarding to Greens. The more that what you want them to do is clearly linked to the establishment and maintenance of meaningful order, the more willing Greens will generally be to engage their strengths in those activities.

Greens will tend to feel more motivated in organized and predictable environments that allow sufficient time for decision-making. They are likely to follow people who are open and clear about what they want, without imposing their wants or feelings on Greens.

To influence Greens, engage them in a conversation about how a desired action will:

- Permit them to pursue their interests without undue outside direction.

- Be fair, practical, and adhere to principles.

- Increase the predictability or reliability of a system or environment.

- Enable the testing of a hypothesis or create a learning experience.

## How to Approach Greens

- Remain objective, logical, fair, and in control of emotions.

- Respect principles and procedures.

- Be prepared to present supportable facts calmly and methodically.

- Ask questions for added clarification, and allow time for considered responses.

- Analyze the impact of potential decisions.

## Things to Avoid when Approaching Greens

- Using broad, unsubstantiated statements or arguments based on emotion.

- Forcing opinions on them, jumping to conclusions, demanding guesses or estimates.

- Rushing discussions and leaving out details.

- Trivializing the need for structure and plans.

- Prying, small talk, inappropriate humor, or forcing help on them.

## Preventing Conflict with Greens

Much conflict with Greens can be prevented by acting or communicating in ways that recognize and respect Greens' MVS and do not introduce conflict triggers. Proactive conflict prevention strategies can be employed to reduce the chance that the self-worth of Greens will be threatened.

- Avoid using broad, unsubstantiated statements or arguments based on emotion.

- Resist making assumptions or jumping to conclusions.

- Be logical and substantive in support of your opinions.

- Allow the need for thoughtful consideration without rushing discussions or leaving out details.

- Be conversationally appropriate, avoiding "small talk" or humor that might be misunderstood.

- Consider the logic of your request or approach, asking questions for clarification.

- Be prepared to present supportable facts calmly, methodically, and unemotionally.

## REWARDING AND RECOGNIZING GREENS

Greens like to be respected for their expertise, reliability, and judgment; they like to know that any structure or system they create is useful to others. Greens generally prefer that rewards and praise be given personally, in private settings or small groups. They may appear to be somewhat independent of the reward structure within which they operate.

The best compliments are specific about being rational and reliable, conserving resources, or preventing difficulties by planning ahead. Some compliments for Greens might include:

- "Your careful, well thought-out plan resulted in our completing the project on time and on budget."

- "Your analysis and recommendations significantly improved the system."

- "Your research saved us from making a serious mistake."

- "Your cool, level-headed approach restored objectivity and saved hours of confusion."

# The Red-Blue MVS
## ASERTIVE-NUTURING

**As·ser·tive**—confidently self-assured and forceful
**Nur·tur·ing**—protecting, supporting, and encouraging others

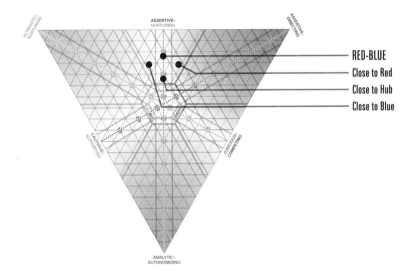

The dot on the SDI triangle represents an individual's Motivational Value System (MVS). Each person's MVS is a combination of three primary motives working together in a unique way showing the frequency with which people are motivated by concerns typical of each motive. This descriptive text is written with an MVS dot located centrally in the Red-Blue MVS region in mind.

Individuals with MVS dots in the Red-Blue MVS region close to the borders (within six points) of other MVS regions may differ slightly from this description. They will likely find that the descriptions of the neighboring region(s) also influence their understanding of themselves and the way they are perceived by others.

## Red-Blue Motives and Values

The motivation of people with an Assertive-Nurturing Motivational Value System (hereafter referred to as Red-Blues) is to achieve feelings of self-worth by actively encouraging others to grow, succeed, and accomplish results together.

Red-Blues tend to find satisfaction in life by identifying needs quickly, then moving swiftly toward bringing assistance to those in need. They feel drawn to mentoring relationships and often defend those perceived as being vulnerable. Red-Blues are focused on the achievement of their goals, while also actively encouraging others to grow and succeed through their guidance. Red-Blues value the power of recognizing and rapidly developing the potential of others.

Red-Blues' sense of personal integrity comes from advocating for the protection, growth, and welfare of others through task accomplishment and leadership. They tend to combine a friendly and direct approach, gaining satisfaction from seeing others move forward and benefit from their coaching. They value decisiveness and are often quick to know what they should do and what others should do. Red-Blues view advice to others as an expression of their concern for others and belief in others' potential.

For Red-Blues, there is a clear understanding of the compassionate use of power and the need to act promptly in matters affecting others' welfare. Red-Blues work hard to earn recognition and appreciation. They tend to be open, enthusiastic, and friendly, demonstrating sincere compassion for others. They are positive and usually want to support initiatives that facilitate the growth and development of others.

## Red-Blue Behaviors

The group of behavioral traits that Red-Blues most frequently use is called the Altruistic-Nurturing Valued Relating Style (VRS). Red-Blues tend to:

- Actively seek opportunities to support others.

- Persuade and energize others, often resulting in the growth and development of others.

- Be open to proposals for creating welfare and security for others.

- Create enthusiasm and support in tackling obstacles to success.

- Be positive, enthusiastic, and forward-thinking.

- Demonstrate sincerity, compassion, and decisiveness.

- Clearly state how goals will benefit others, and make decisions on their behalf.

- Recognize the importance of results *and* the needs of others.

- Be direct, friendly, and action-oriented.

Red-Blue strengths confirm the self-worth of both people in a relationship. When Red-Blue strengths are overdone, they may threaten the self-worth of Red-Blues or other people who perceive these strengths as overdone. Table 2.4 illustrates two examples:

**Table 2.4** *Examples of Red-Blue Overdone Strengths*

| Productive Strength | Effect of Overdone Strength |
|---|---|
| When Red-Blues are enthusiastic, they can inspire others to overcome obstacles and become more successful. | When Red-Blues are overly enthusiastic, they may disregard information or push people to act before they are ready. |
| When Red-Blues are compassionate, they accurately assess and meet the needs of others. | When the compassion of Red-Blues is focused on people before they are ready, it can be viewed as pressuring and intrusive. |

## How Red-Blues Enter Conflict

Red-Blues tend to go into conflict about things that impede or delay progress, especially when rules or processes get in the way of doing the right thing for others. They have difficulty with people who are self-serving or stand by idly when others are in need. Awareness of the potential causes of conflict can help Red-Blues to manage their own reactions to conflict triggers and can help others adjust their behavior in an attempt to prevent conflict.

Red-Blues may experience conflict when they perceive any of the following conflict triggers:

- Other people are negative about options and possibilities, refusing to get involved.

- Too much time or detail is required before a decision can be made.

- Others are being taken advantage of, disregarded, blamed, or excluded.

- Their involvement and/or contributions are asked for and then ignored.

- Others refuse to get involved, withholding support for people who could truly benefit.

- Others behave indifferently, seeming to ignore or take for granted the hard work and dedication of Red-Blues.

- The people around them perceive Red-Blue assertiveness as aggression, making accusations that Red-Blues are exploiting others for their own means.

- They feel isolated or left out of what is happening.

- The guidance they offer is not accepted, but instead challenged or even rejected.

- Plans that could lead to others' success are overruled, and the human cost of decisions is ignored.

When in conflict, Red-Blues want to defend their values, so they can get back to relating to others productively. The way they defend their MVS in an effort to return to feeling good about themselves will vary, depending on their Conflict Sequence.

## PRODUCTIVE RESULTS OF CONFLICT FOR RED-BLUES

When in conflict, regardless of their individual different Conflict Sequences, Red-Blues share a desire to return to feelings of self-worth and activities that develop others. They are more likely to resolve conflict when they see the potential for some of these outcomes:

- Harmony, openness, and straight-talk in the relationship will be quickly restored.

- Barriers to development will be overcome or removed.

- Others will feel valued, because their needs were clearly considered during conflict resolution.

- People who have been disadvantaged will be given equal access to resources or opportunities.

- A renewed and blame-free commitment to each other is established, even in the face of future adversity.

## How Red-Blues Can Borrow Behavior for Increased Effectiveness

Red-Blues' preferred approach to situations and other people may not always result in outcomes that are valuable to Red-Blues or to others. Mentoring strengths may not fit certain situations, or they may be perceived as overdone, possibly triggering conflict in others. Borrowing behavior is most effective when considering the MVS of others, and advice about how to approach people with different Motivational Value Systems can be found in the other MVS sections of this book.

Red-Blues may carry the burdens of pride from Red and guilt from Blue. Red-Blues are driven by leading others to get the best results in their lives. Red-Blues take great satisfaction in quickly being able to feel what "the best" is. If that help should fail or be perceived as meddling Red-Blues may feel guilty because the right result was not achieved. In addition, they may feel discouraged, because they should have known how to best advise others.

Red-Blues may sometimes relate more effectively with others by borrowing non-preferred behavior, such as:

- Taking time to assess whether others actually require input or advice before offering advice or help.

- Softening the intensity and directness of communication to ensure that an assertive style does not hide the nurturing intent.

- Pausing, giving others time to think, and listening fully to others before responding.

- Methodically considering the steps required to achieve a goal, without offering too many ideas too quickly.

- Setting opinions about others' best interest aside momentarily and listen carefully to what others desire.

- Calculating the risks inherent in a course of action and becoming more cautious about when to offer support.

## THE RED-BLUE STYLE OF PERSONAL LEADERSHIP AND INFLUENCE

When leading others, Red-Blues tend to focus on coaching or mentoring others, believing that by providing assistance, encouragement, and challenges, others will rise to higher levels of engagement and performance. Red-Blues view the purpose of leadership as directing others for the benefit of those others. The Red-Blue leadership style is energetic and charismatic, inspiring people to create a better future that meets the needs of people. Their leadership will be characterized by:

- Seeking opportunities to mentor and coach others.

- Celebrating accomplishments and successes.

- Advising others on how to be their best by actively providing feedback to improve their lives, professionally and personally.

- Focusing others on finding and seizing opportunities.

- Giving extra support to the disadvantaged or overlooked.

# Working with Red-Blues

## INFLUENCING RED-BLUES

The key to influencing Red-Blues is to create or communicate conditions that are intrinsically rewarding to Red-Blues. The more what you want them to do is clearly linked to the protection, growth, and welfare of others through task accomplishment, the more willing Red-Blues will be to engage their strengths in those activities.

Red-Blues will tend to feel more motivated in enthusiastic, open, compassionate, and growth-oriented environments. They are likely to follow people who share their power with others, rather than exercise their power over others.

To influence Red-Blues, engage them in a conversation about how a desired action will:

- Create security and well-being for others.

- Generate enthusiasm and buy-in for others to overcome obstacles.

- Result in appreciation and respect from people who benefit from their actions.

- Give an advantage to people who deserve it.

## How to Approach Red-Blues

- Be positive, enthusiastic, open, and forward-thinking.

- Demonstrate sincerity, compassion, and decisiveness.

- Clearly state how goals will benefit others.

- Recognize the importance of results and the needs of others.

- Keep it direct, simple, friendly, and action-oriented.

## Things to Avoid when Approaching Red-Blues

- Being negative, indecisive, apathetic, or refusing to get involved.

- Over-emphasizing process, details, or rules.

- Lacking enthusiasm or focus.

- Disregarding the needs of others, taking advantage of others, or putting self-interest first.

- Ignoring or diminishing their involvement or contributions.

## Preventing Conflict with Red-Blues

Much conflict with Red-Blues can be prevented by acting or communicating in ways that recognize and respect Red-Blues' MVS and do not introduce conflict triggers. Proactive conflict prevention strategies can be employed to reduce the chance that the self-worth of Red-Blues will be threatened.

- Emphasize that you understand how important the issue is to them and that you are committed to solving the problem.

- Demonstrate an understanding of Red-Blues' intent to benefit others through action.

- Clarify that maintaining the relationship is just as important as solving any problem.

- Use energy in your response, reflecting back an understanding of the urgency around finding solutions.

- Don't make commitments lightly or change an agreed-upon course of action.

## REWARDING AND RECOGNIZING RED-BLUES

Red-Blues like to be known for their compassion and their ability to improve the lives of others through advice, coaching, or direct intervention. Red-Blues tend to like both public and private recognition and also enjoy seeing the people they helped earn rewards and recognition.

The best compliments are specific about the advice, challenge, or support that led a person or a group to improve. Some compliments for Red-Blues might include:

- "We would have never overcome those obstacles without your enthusiasm, hard work, and support."

- "You always know exactly what I need."

- "I admire the way you build other people up; it really makes a difference here."

- "It's so inspiring, the way you recognize talent in people that others miss."

- "You really encouraged people to do their best."

- "It was great to see how people worked so well together under your direction."

- "People will really benefit from your efforts."

# The Red-Green MVS

## JUDICIOUS-COMPETING

**Ju·di·cious**—having, showing, or being done with good judgment or sense
**Com·pet·ting**—striving to gain or win by doing something better than others

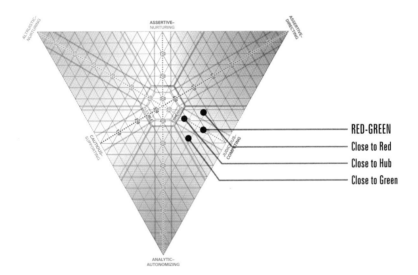

The dot on the SDI triangle represents an individual's Motivational Value System (MVS). Each person's MVS is a combination of three primary motives working together in a unique way showing the frequency with which people are motivated by concerns typical of each motive. This descriptive text is written with an MVS dot located centrally in the Red-Green MVS region in mind.

Individuals with MVS dots in the Red-Green MVS region close to the borders (within six points) of other MVS regions may differ slightly from this description. They will likely find that the descriptions of the neighboring region(s) also influence their understanding of themselves and the way they are perceived by others.

# Red-Green Motives and Values

The motivation of people with a Judicious-Competing Motivational Value System (hereafter referred to as Red-Greens) is to achieve feelings of self-worth by using carefully thought-out strategies to achieve ambitious and rational objectives.

Red-Greens tend to find satisfaction in life by providing rational leadership that assesses risk and opportunity, integrating those components into elegantly planned victories. Red-Greens' self-worth is affirmed by the efficient execution of logical plans and complex strategies. The accomplishment process must be logical, and the achievement of desired goals must come through an orderly action plan. Red-Greens value the power of systemic, strategic planning and implementation.

Red-Greens' sense of personal integrity comes from using strategies and efficient tactics to maximize the use of resources. They are supportive and loyal to those who will help them, without hesitation or qualification, to be successful. They integrate planning and implementation, viewing the concepts as virtually indistinguishable.

For Red-Greens, there is a clear understanding of the rational use of power and the desire to act promptly with good judgment in matters affecting their competitive edge. Red-Greens tend to be strong and principled. They want to earn recognition and respect. They feel responsible for developing and leading winning strategies, and they want to direct others in an impartial, efficient manner.

# Red-Green Behaviors

The group of behavioral traits that Red-Greens most frequently use is called the Judicious-Competing Valued Relating Style (VRS). Red-Greens tend to:

- Provide rational leadership that can assess risks and opportunities.

- Be decisive and proactive when all the facts are in.

- Challenge opposition through thoughtful process and strategy.

- Demonstrate understanding of the situation, and get to the point deliberately.

- Have facts available to support a winning strategy.

- Confidently communicate relevant facts that lead to justifiable action.

- Compete against others and against their own past performances.

- Be challenging, realistic, and open to a well-thought out response.

- Think strategically and logically.

- Defend logical positions with energy and forcefulness.

Red-Green strengths confirm the self-worth of both people in a relationship. When Red-Green strengths are overdone, they may threaten the self-worth of Red-Greens or other people who perceive these strengths as overdone. Table 2.5 illustrates two examples:

**Table 2.5** *Examples of Red-Green Overdone Strengths*

| Productive Strength | Effect of Overdone Strength |
|---|---|
| When Red-Greens compete toward shared goals or objectives, everyone benefits from the success. | When Red-Greens are overly competitive, they may disregard how others feel about the goals. |
| When Red-Greens are strategic, they can identify the most efficient method of accomplishing something. | When Red-Greens are overly strategic, their methods may be viewed as manipulative or self-serving. |

## How Red-Greens Enter Conflict

Red-Greens tend to go into conflict about things that block their ability to plan or implement logical plans. They have difficulty with people who give up too easily, who are overly emotional, intrusive, or who think illogically. Awareness of the potential causes of conflict can help Red-Greens manage their own reactions to conflict triggers and can help others adjust their behavior in an attempt to prevent conflict.

Red-Greens may experience conflict when they perceive any of the following conflict triggers:

- They are required to slow down for what they determine to be an invalid reason.

- An important decision is being made without adequate thought and analysis, possibly resulting in a rash or unexpected result.

- There is too much emphasis on the interpersonal aspects of a task.

- Others are behaving in an impulsive or emotional way.

- Logic is overlooked in the planning process.

- They are treated with passivity or ignorance.

- Others perceive their choices as mindless or aggressive.

- They are operating in an environment that does not recognize achievement or an environment where achievement is difficult to quantify.

- They must comply with a system that requires unnecessary steps.

- They are being forced to operate within the constraints of rules that are illogical or counterproductive.

When in conflict, Red-Greens want to defend their values, so they can get back to relating to others productively. The way they defend their MVS in an effort to return to feeling good about themselves will vary, depending on their Conflict Sequence.

## PRODUCTIVE RESULTS OF CONFLICT FOR RED-GREENS

When in conflict, regardless of their individual different Conflict Sequences, Red-Greens share a desire to return to feelings of self-worth and activities that are rational and strategic. They are more likely to resolve conflict when they see the potential for some of these outcomes:

- Quick, clear action will be supported by a logical plan.

- Better alignment will be achieved, because the thinking behind the action will be understood and accepted.

- Appropriate but not excessive time will be allocated to develop an action plan.

- Problems will be solved efficiently and without emotion so resolution will be both fair and actionable.

- Goals will be clarified, so the conversation can shift to methods.

## How Red-Greens Can Borrow Behavior
## for Increased Effectiveness

Red-Greens' preferred approach to situations and other people may not always result in outcomes that are valuable to Red-Greens or to others. Red-Green strengths may not fit certain situations, or they may be perceived as overdone, possibly triggering conflict in others. Borrowing behavior is most effective when considering the MVS of others, and advice about how to approach people with different Motivational Value Systems can be found in the other MVS sections of this book.

Red-Greens may bear the burdens of pride from Red and certainty from Green. When they develop strategies to achieve desired results, they analyze situations and logically craft their approaches. The Green in the blend contributes certainty that these approaches are the correct ways to solve problems and get outcomes. The Red in the blend adds great pride in a history of developing excellent and pragmatic solutions. When Red-Greens encounter a failure of their strategies, they have to face the reality that not only were they incorrect, but that they also lost. Pride and certainty together make it difficult for Red-Greens to objectively assess their positions and remain open to others' ideas about improvement.

Red-Greens may sometimes relate more effectively with others by borrowing non-preferred behavior, such as:

- Taking time to check in with people on a personal level.

- Making people's issues or the affect on people part of every strategy.

- Being tolerant of people who are not focused primarily on the big picture.

- Accepting the suggestions of others as tentative revisions to collaboratively explore.

- Including all people who could be affected in planning processes.

- Recognizing and rewarding people for meeting expectations, rather than only for exceeding expectations.

## The Red-Green Style of Personal Leadership and Influence

When leading others, Red-Greens tend to focus on the effective execution of plans, believing that a clear strategy is a mandate for action. Red-Greens view the purpose of leadership as rationally using power to increase the probability of success. The Red-Green leadership style is precise, principled, and decisive when the facts are in, optimizing resources and overpowering obstacles to assure victory. Their leadership style will be characterized by:

- Figuring all the angles and developing winning strategies.

- Organizing commitment and resources to get to the goal in the most streamlined manner.

- Building the capacity of an organization for low maintenance and high performance.

- Seeking tactical leverage points to multiply the effects of people's efforts and invested resources.

# Working with Red-Greens

## Influencing Red-Greens

The key to influencing Red-Greens is to create or communicate conditions that are intrinsically rewarding to Red-Greens. The more what you want them to do is clearly linked to strategic accomplishment and fairness in competition, the more willing Red-Greens will generally be to engage their strengths in those activities.

Red-Greens will tend to feel more motivated in complex, challenging environments that offer opportunities to calculate, compete, and win. They are likely to follow people who are supportive and loyal and who will help them achieve success.

To influence Red-Greens, engage them in a conversation about how a desired action will:

- Allow them to craft and implement strategy.

- Improve their ability to compete.

- Enable them to fully survey the risks and potential rewards in a situation.

- Engage them in a rational challenge.

## How to Approach Red-Greens

- Demonstrate understanding of the situation, and get to the point quickly.

- Have facts readily available to support a winning strategy.

- Confidently communicate relevant facts that lead to justifiable action.

- Be challenging, realistic, and open.

- Think strategically, logically, and impartially.

## Things to Avoid when Approaching Red-Greens

- Emotional decision-making or personalizing issues.

- Being passive, uninvolved, ambivalent, or vague.

- Giving in or giving up, unless there's a logical reason to do so.

- Accepting everything without challenging anything.

- Resisting logical solutions and related actions for emotional reasons.

## Preventing Conflict with Red-Greens

Much conflict with Red-Greens can be prevented by acting or communicating in ways that recognize and respect Red-Greens' MVS and do not introduce conflict triggers. Proactive conflict prevention strategies can be employed to reduce the chance the self-worth of Red-Greens will be threatened.

- Be unemotional and direct.

- Own your role in the interaction, and calmly explain the reasons behind the behaviors chosen.

- Discuss the thought processes that decisions are based upon before action is taken.

- If challenged, be prepared to stand and engage with the analysis.

- Know your position, and be prepared to defend it rationally.

## Rewarding and Recognizing Red-Greens

Red-Greens like to be valued for their pragmatic and strategic skills and their ability to condense large volumes of information into actionable plans. Red-Greens prefer that rewards be clearly structured and administered, so they can control the inputs to the system and justifiably claim the rewards.

The best compliments are about the design or implementation of strategy and the specific results that were produced. Some compliments for Red-Greens might include:

- "That was elegantly planned and masterfully executed."

- "Your strategic insight into the challenge made it possible for us to close the deal."

- "Your analytical work and sheer force of will made the difference between success and failure."

- "You saw the opportunity in a complex situation and turned it to our advantage, while everyone else only saw the risks."

# The Blue-Green MVS

## CAUTIOUS-SUPPORTING

**Cau·tious**—careful to avoid potential problems or dangers
**Sup·port·ing**—providing encouragement, comfort, and emotional help

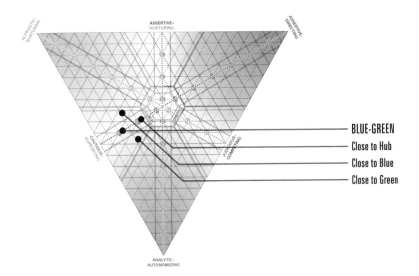

The dot on the SDI triangle represents an individual's Motivational Value System (MVS). Each person's MVS is a combination of three primary motives working together in a unique way, showing the frequency with which people are motivated by concerns typical of each motive. This descriptive text is written with an MVS dot located centrally in the Blue-Green MVS region in mind.

Individuals with MVS dots in the Blue-Green MVS region close to the borders (within six points) of other MVS regions may differ slightly from this description. They will likely find that the descriptions of the neighboring region(s) also influence their understanding of themselves and the way they are perceived by others.

## BLUE-GREEN MOTIVES AND VALUES

The motivation of people with a Cautious-Supporting Motivational Value System (hereafter referred to as Blue-Greens) is to achieve feelings of self-worth by being genuinely helpful to others while maintaining self-sufficiency for both themselves and the people they help.

Blue-Greens tend to find satisfaction in life through accurately assessing other people's needs and contributing to their self-reliance. Blue-Greens value giving assistance to people who are genuinely in need of help and are willing to utilize the help offered. Blue-Greens tend to understand and value the productivity behind moving quietly to the aid of others with an efficient plan. Blue-Greens tend to believe in prudent helpfulness, setting limits on assistance to others in order to develop their self-sufficiency. Blue-Greens value the power of building the capacity of self and others.

Blue-Greens' sense of personal integrity comes from creating fair processes that help people become self-reliant. For Blue-Greens, the real measure of success is how helpful they can be without threatening their own sense of independence or the independence of those they are helping. Blue-Greens believe in the balance of principles and feelings, of logic and emotion. Blue-Greens tend to feel rewarded when their well-planned help brings out the best in others.

For Blue-Greens, life is often about clearly understanding the use of feelings and reason to better the welfare and independence of others. Blue-Greens tend to alert others to risks they may not have considered. Blue-Greens prefer a conscientious, patient environment that respects the feelings of others and adheres to fair principles.

## BLUE-GREEN BEHAVIORS

The group of behavioral traits that Blue-Greens most frequently use is called the Cautious-Supporting Valued Relating Style (VRS). Blue-Greens tend to:

- Be patient, soft-spoken, and conscientious when relating with others.

- Be fair, logical, and principled in the consideration of other people's needs.

- Help people who truly need or deserve help and who will be able to help themselves later.

- Quietly move to the aid of others using both feelings and reason.

- Defend the rights and values of others.

- Nurture the growth of other people's self-reliance through an analysis of their needs.

- Be warm and principled, combining compassion and logic to guide others.

- Be reserved and cautious about expressing their own needs, refraining from self-assertion.

- Limit the amount of help provided to others to maintain their own independence.

- Want to be included in decisions about matters affecting the welfare of others.

Blue-Green strengths confirm the self-worth of both people in a relationship. When Blue-Green strengths are overdone, they may threaten the self-worth of Blue-Greens or other people who perceive these strengths as overdone. Table 2.6 illustrates two examples:

**Table 2.6** *Examples of Blue-Green Overdone Strengths*

| Productive Strength | Effect of Overdone Strength |
|---|---|
| When Blue-Greens are self-sufficient, they can be productive without imposing on others. | When Blue-Greens are overly self-sufficient, they may refuse assistance and become isolated from others. |
| When Blue-Greens thoughtfully support others, they guide them toward future independence. | When Blue-Greens are overly supportive, they may sacrifice their own needs in the continued service of others. |

## How Blue-Greens Enter Conflict

Blue-Greens tend to go into conflict about things that block their ability to thoughtfully encourage growth and independence or systematically bring forth the best in others. They have difficulty with people who impose their will, help, or principles on others. Awareness of the potential causes of conflict can help

Blue-Greens to manage their own reactions to conflict triggers and can help others adjust their behavior in an attempt to prevent conflict.

Blue-Greens may experience conflict when they perceive any of the following conflict triggers:

- Others are being intrusive, confrontational, or invading their personal space.

- They are being pushed to move ahead before they are ready.

- People appear to be braggarts and meddlers, who presume upon and compete with others in any situation.

- They are being treated with anger or disdain and are accused of fostering child-like dependence.

- They are being pushed for an answer without being allowed time to think.

- Solutions are being dictated, and power is being used to force outcomes.

- Interactions with others are not carefully thought out, lacking the analysis to appropriately aid those who might be in need.

- Change is required before the rational justification of the *need* for that change is satisfactorily proven, and before the impact the change will make on others is duly considered.

- They are being pressured to get involved in something that may result in a high, personal cost to them.

- Clarification of issues and emotions is blocked, forcing action without reflective discussion.

When in conflict, Blue-Greens want to defend their values, so they can get back to relating to others productively. The way they defend their MVS in an effort to return to feeling good about themselves will vary, depending on their Conflict Sequence.

## PRODUCTIVE RESULTS OF CONFLICT FOR BLUE-GREENS

When in conflict, regardless of their individual different Conflict Sequences, Blue-Greens share a desire to return to feelings of self-worth and activities that are rational and compassionate. They are more likely to resolve conflict when they see the potential for some of these outcomes:

- Balance between the problem's solution and the emotions related to the problem will be maintained.

- People who truly need and deserve help will get it.

- Expectations and boundaries will be clarified.

- Principles that were disregarded by others during the conflict will be reaffirmed and protected.

- Self-sufficiency of others and themselves will be re-established.

## How Blue-Greens Can Borrow Behavior for Increased Effectiveness

Blue-Greens' preferred approach to situations and other people may not always result in outcomes that are valuable to Blue-Greens or to others. Cautious strengths may not fit certain situations, or they may be perceived as overdone, possibly triggering conflict in others. Borrowing behavior is most effective when considering the MVS of others, and advice about how to approach people with different Motivational Value Systems can be found in the other MVS sections of this book.

Blue-Greens may bear the burden of guilt from Blue and certainty from Green. Blue-Greens feel gratified when they can accurately assess others' needs and create solutions that help them become more self-sufficient. When Blue-Greens create plans to help, they analyze situations and try to deliver just the right amount of help to make a sustainable difference for the other person. The Green in the blend is certain that the plan is logically appropriate for the need. When such a plan does not work as expected and, therefore, does not help as planned, Blue-Greens may feel discouraged that they wasted their efforts and were incorrect. They may also feel guilty, because help was not provided.

Blue-Greens may sometimes relate more effectively with others by borrowing non-preferred behavior such as:

- Clearly and assertively stating personal preferences and desires.

- Taking small risks as a way of testing plans.

- Offering opinions about things without being asked.

- Clarifying the urgency and importance of tasks with others.

- Being bold and decisive when the course of action is clear.

- Being forceful and persuasive in the defense of the rights of self and others.

## THE BLUE-GREEN STYLE OF PERSONAL LEADERSHIP AND INFLUENCE

When leading others, Blue-Greens tend to focus on creating structures and environments that facilitate self-reliance, believing that the people they lead are capable of making excellent decisions. Blue-Greens view the purpose of leadership as enabling others to act independently and responsibly. The Blue-Green leadership style is calm and contemplative, using analysis to minimize risk and maximize personal and professional development. Their leadership will be characterized by:

- Establishing systems that help others become self-reliant.

- Creating an environment in which people can be authentic and productive.

- Serving the needs of people who are implementing the vision.

- Quietly moving to the aid of others, using feelings and reason to guide their approach.

# Working with Blue-Greens

## INFLUENCING BLUE-GREENS

The key to influencing Blue-Greens is to create or communicate conditions that are intrinsically rewarding to Blue-Greens. The more what you want them to do is clearly linked to social justice or the establishment and maintenance of self-sufficiency, the more willing Blue-Greens will generally be to engage their strengths in those activities.

Blue-Greens will tend to feel more motivated in fair, conscientious, and respectful environments that thoughtfully bring out the best in others. They are likely to follow people who are cautious, rational, and respectful and thorough in whatever they do.

To influence Blue-Greens, engage them in a conversation about how a desired action will:

- Provide learning and guidance for others.

- Create processes that will protect others or enhance their well-being.

- Bring out the best in others.

- Enable them to systematically support people who need support.

## How to Approach Blue-Greens

- Be calm, patient, open, and genuine.

- Be considerate and respectful of others' space and of their processing time.

- Ask their opinion before sharing your own.

- Offer logical proposals without pushing too assertively.

- Emphasize principles and fairness, and recognize how the process will affect others.

## Things to Avoid when Approaching Blue-Greens

- Bragging or being overly enthusiastic or confident.

- Being intrusive and confrontational, or speaking loudly.

- Violating their personal space.

- Pushing them to engage before they are ready, without appropriate time to think about the outcomes.

- Forcing them to compete with others or appearing to take advantage of others.

## Preventing Conflict with Blue-Greens

Much conflict with Blue-Greens can be prevented by acting or communicating in ways that recognize and respect Blue-Greens' MVS and do not introduce conflict triggers. Proactive conflict prevention strategies can be employed to reduce the chance that the self-worth of Blue-Greens will be threatened.

- Avoid raised voices and appearing aggressive or confrontational.

- Be calm and logical in support of your opinions, while keeping an eye on the relationship cost of any potential disagreement.

- Allow time for thoughtful consideration without rushing ahead or forcing compliance.

- Resist isolating them from others or being indecisive in matters that affect their welfare.

- Depersonalize the problem, and reassure them that the relationship matters.

- Consider the logic of your request and how that request will impact others involved in the situation.

- Make a genuine inquiry about their welfare and how the situation is affecting them.

## REWARDING AND RECOGNIZING BLUE-GREENS

Blue-Greens like to be recognized for their self-reliance and for maintaining environments where others are able to grow and act independently. Blue-Greens appreciate reasonable and justifiable rewards that are shared fairly with all of those who contributed to success.

The best compliments tend to be specific about providing structured guidance, protecting the rights of others, or avoiding problems by anticipating and addressing potential risks. Some compliments for Blue-Greens might include:

- "Your careful, well thought-out plan made a positive difference for the people involved."

- "You gave me just enough help and just enough space so that I was able to finish it myself."

- "Your patience and willingness to work with others resulted in a sustainable solution."

- "Thank you. Your calm, careful approach allowed us to stop that from becoming a problem and to maintain harmony on the team."

# The Hub MVS

## FLEXIBLE-COHERING

**Flex·i·ble**—able to respond to changing circumstances and conditions
**Co·her·ing**—bringing together to form a united whole

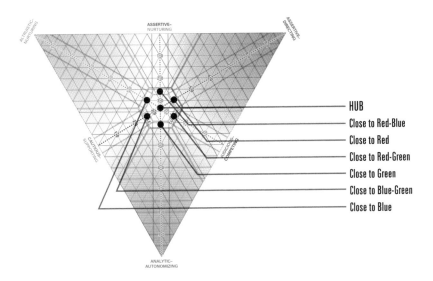

The dot on the SDI triangle represents an individual's Motivational Value System (MVS). Each person's MVS is a combination of three primary motives working together in a unique way showing the frequency with which people are motivated by concerns typical of each motive. This descriptive text is written with an MVS dot located centrally in the Hub MVS region in mind.

Individuals with MVS dots in the Hub MVS region close to the borders (within six points) of other MVS regions may differ slightly from this description. They will likely find that the descriptions of the neighboring region(s) also influence their understanding of themselves and the way they are perceived by others.

## Hub Motives and Values

The motivation of people with a Flexible-Cohering Motivational Value System (hereafter referred to as Hubs) is to achieve feelings of self-worth by finding and meeting the needs of groups, remaining open to seeing all sides of situations, and working with others in ways that are appropriate to various situations.

Hubs tend to find satisfaction in life by being flexible in approach and responsive and adaptable in relating to others. They collect information about the needs of the group in order to find common ground and meet the group's needs. Hubs want to see all sides of a situation, demonstrating empathy with a variety of different types of people, situations, and challenges. Hubs can be described as tolerant, social, creative, and versatile. They value the power of sharing perspective and building consensus.

Hubs' sense of personal integrity comes from exercising their ability to read situations and respond to them in situationally appropriate means. Hubs strive to meet the needs of the moment while maintaining future flexibility. Hubs tend to promote cohesiveness by getting others together to share ideas and consider alternatives. They want to unite people in a common cause, and they are willing to play whatever role is necessary to do so.

For Hubs, there is a desire to coordinate their efforts with others in some common undertaking that involves closeness, clear lines of authority, and opportunities for self-reliance. Hubs want to be good team members and loyal followers who know how to exercise authority, when to follow the rules, and when to use good judgment. They tend to be friendly, democratic, and playful. Hubs value building consensus through encouraging interactions and exploring points of view.

## Hub Behaviors

The group of behavioral traits that Hubs most frequently use is called the Flexible-Cohering Valued Relating Style (VRS). Hubs tend to:

- Be curious about what others think and feel.

- Be open-minded and willing to adapt.

- Experiment with different ways of behaving.

- Be flexible, social, playful, and collaborative.

- Maintain an appropriate balance between process, people, and performance.

- Include other people, and recognize their contributions.

- Remain open to new ideas, options, and possibilities.

- Examine the situation from multiple perspectives.

- Have multiple goals and more than one area of focus.

- Use social skills and personal charm to cope with realities in the world.

Hub strengths confirm the self-worth of both people in a relationship. When Hub strengths are overdone, they may threaten the self-worth of Hubs or other people who perceive these strengths as overdone. Table 2.7 illustrates two examples:

**Table 2.7** *Examples of Hub Overdone Strengths*

| Productive Strength | Effect of Overdone Strength |
| --- | --- |
| When Hubs are flexible, they can assess a situation from multiple perspectives and aid in collective understanding. | When Hubs are overly flexible, they can agree with different things at different times, which appears inconsistent and unpredictable. |
| When Hubs are curious, they bring novel and useful ideas to relationships and situations that others may have missed. | When Hubs are overly curious, they may be easily distracted by options and lose focus on the current situation |

## How Hubs Enter Conflict

Hubs tend to go into conflict about things that block their flexibility or restrict their options until the best solution or plan is developed. They have difficulty with people who don't participate in group activities or who do not see the merit of reconsidering plans when new information is known. Awareness of the potential causes of conflict can help Hubs to manage their own reactions to conflict triggers and can help others adjust their behavior in an attempt to prevent conflict.

Hubs may experience conflict when they perceive any of the following conflict triggers:

- They must operate in an environment that doesn't allow enough time to explore the opinions of others.

- Others restrict their ability to change, insisting only one approach or solution.

- They are required to interact with others who are strict, unyielding, or domineering.

- Others are excluded from the group or treated indifferently.

- Consensus-building is not valued or allowed.

- They are not being heard, or they fear that their input is unwelcome or undesirable.

- They are managed in a style that rewards compliance and does not value their innovative efforts and contributions.

- They are being locked into a rigid and inflexible future without any opportunity to reconsider or reevaluate their options.

- They can see that several mutually exclusive opportunities have equal value, and it is not clear that any one of them is better than the others.

When in conflict, Hubs want to defend their values, so they can get back to relating to others productively. The way they defend their MVS in an effort to return to feeling good about themselves will vary, depending on their Conflict Sequence.

## PRODUCTIVE RESULTS OF CONFLICT FOR HUBS

When in conflict, regardless of their individual different Conflict Sequences, Hubs share a desire to return to feelings of self-worth and activities that are inclusive and flexible. They are more likely to resolve conflict when they see the potential for some of these outcomes:

- Consensus will lead to implementation of the best possible solution for the situation.

- There will be restored flexibility in approach and an agreement to revisit plans when new information is available.

- There will be effective and fun-filled collaboration among those involved in the situation.

- People will be open-minded about alternative solutions, as well as feelings about those solutions.

- People will be included, and a sense of camaraderie and shared purpose will be created.

## How Hubs Can Borrow Behavior for Increased Effectiveness

Hubs' preferred approach to situations and other people may not always result in outcomes that are valuable to Hubs or to others. Adaptable strengths may not fit certain situations, or they may be perceived as overdone, possibly triggering conflict in others. Borrowing behavior is most effective when considering the MVS of others, and advice about how to approach people with different Motivational Value Systems can be found in the other MVS sections of this book.

Hubs have all three primary motivations blended about equally; they may carry the burdens of guilt from Blue, pride from Red, and certainty from Green. These integrated colors may also cause additional challenges. Hubs may bear the burden of appropriateness, the desire to be whatever someone (or a situation) needs them to be. They may lose their true sense of self by constantly checking the appropriateness of their behavior with others. Hubs also may find maintaining focus and making a decision that eliminates other options to be frustrating.

Hubs may sometimes relate more effectively with others by borrowing non-preferred behavior such as:

- Discussing contingencies with others, as well as the types of new information that would require reconsideration of an agreement.

- Setting and disclose deadlines for decisions.

- Selecting any option and act on it in situations where all options seem equally attractive.

- Describing the process that led to a decision, so others can be aware of the internal logic and how it fits the situation.

- Clearly articulating the principles and critical issues that will remain constant in their decision-making process.

- Clearly and assertively stating personal preferences.

## The Hub Style of Personal Leadership and Influence

When leading others, Hubs tend to focus on creating an inclusive environment that fosters collaboration and consensus, believing that the best ideas will come from the synergy of diverse perspectives. Hubs view the purpose of leadership as adapting to and responding appropriately to each situation. The Hub leadership style is flexible and team-based, finding and filling in the gaps, then moving back to the periphery to assess the next move. Their leadership will be characterized by:

- Keeping options open until the most appropriate or most widely acceptable one can be identified and implemented.

- Focusing on the group, making sure that everyone is included and that work is playful and social.

- Valuing creativity, problem-solving, and novelty.

- Being open to contrasting opinions and the relative merits embodied in different points of view.

# Working with Hubs

## Influencing Hubs

The key to influencing Hubs is to create or communicate conditions that are intrinsically rewarding to Hubs. The more what you want them to do is linked to current and future flexibility and the welfare of the group and its members, the more willing Hubs will generally be to engage their strengths in those activities.

Hubs will tend to feel more motivated in democratic, playful, and social environments that encourage consensus. They are likely to follow people who are appropriately balanced, who are generous, strong, and patient.

To influence Hubs, engage them in a conversation about how a desired action will:

- Enable them to use their judgment based on the situation.

- Let them alternate between leading and following, depending on the circumstances.

- Encourage the solicitation of points of view and perspectives.

- Involve others in a collaborative endeavor.

## How to Approach Hubs

- Be flexible, sociable, playful, and collaborative.

- Maintain an appropriate balance between process, people, and goals.

- Include other people, and recognize their contributions.

- Remain open to new ideas, options, and possibilities.

- Examine the situation from multiple perspectives.

## Things to Avoid when Approaching Hubs

- Disregarding group camaraderie or the opinions of others.

- Accepting the first option without hearing others.

- Restricting the ability to change, insisting on only one approach or solution.

- Being strict, unyielding, or domineering.

- Excluding people or being inconsiderate of others.

## Preventing Conflict with Hubs

Much conflict with Hubs can be prevented by acting or communicating in ways that recognize and respect Hubs' MVS and that do not introduce conflict triggers. Proactive conflict prevention strategies can be employed to reduce the chance that the self-worth of Hubs will be threatened.

- Remain open to various ideas, allowing flexibility in the approach to solutions.

- Focus on the attributes of a situation and the different perspectives that people have about it.

- Keep your sense of humor.

- Use a collaborative style to get valuable input into the process.

- Set aside preconceived notions, and explore the possibilities.

## REWARDING AND RECOGNIZING HUBS

Hubs like to be appreciated for responding appropriately to people's needs in the moment, being flexible with regard to tasks, and being tolerant with regards to people. Hubs prefer to be rewarded as part of a group, and if rewarded individually, for their contributions to the group. Some compliments for Hubs might include:

- "You are a natural translator, helping us all to understand each other's perspectives."

- "Thanks for filling in. We know we can always count on you to step in and do whatever is needed for the team."

- "You always seem to be able to sense what's going on around you and then do whatever is appropriate in the situation."

- "The recent decisions you made will give us a lot more flexibility in the future."

# CONFLICT SEQUENCES

# What is a Conflict Sequence?

A Conflict Sequence (CS) is, as its name suggests, an order or pattern of conflict. In SDI terms, a Conflict Sequence is the order in which a person experiences Blue (harmony-seeking), Red (outcome-seeking), and Green (logic-seeking) motivations during the course of conflict.

**Figure 3.1** *The 13 Conflict Sequences*

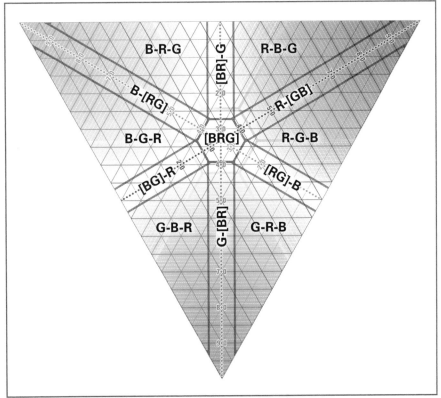

A Conflict Sequence is a consistent pattern of motivational changes during conflict. Motives give purpose and meaning to activities and relationships, and differences in motives during conflict are a significant part of personality. A Conflict Sequence is a simple and practical way of thinking about people and personality types from the perspective of interrelated motives, the complex reasons why people do the things they do when they are faced with conflict.[1]

While all people share a desire to feel good about themselves and to experience feelings of self-worth, all people also experience threats to their sense of self-worth. A threat to self-worth is a definitive characteristic of conflict, and these threats can be real or perceived. Different people experience these threats in different ways.

While everyone is assumed to have all three motives (Blue, Red, and Green), the motives may be experienced in different orders as conflict progresses. The different combinations produce 13 distinct personality types, as described in detail in the following pages. Nine of them have a single color in first stage, three more have two colors blended in stages one and two, and one [BRG] has all three colors blended in all three stages.

The scores from the conflict portion of the SDI are charted as an arrowhead on the SDI triangle to represent a person's Conflict Sequence. The location of the arrowhead suggests one of the 13 Conflict Sequences. However, when an arrowhead is close to another region (within six points[2] as illustrated in Figure 3.2), the person may identify with portions

**Figure 3.2** *Example of 6 Point Test/Retest*

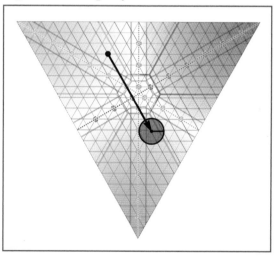

of the descriptions for more than one Conflict Sequence. Unlike a typecasting exercise, the goal is not to force a person to choose only one of the descriptions. Instead, the goal is to allow the individual the flexibility to identify the most characteristic portions of each description.

# WHAT DOES THE CONFLICT SEQUENCE DO?

Motives during conflict give rise to conflict behaviors. As the motives undergo changes, so do the behaviors.[3] One motive that everyone shares during conflict is the desire to return to feeling good again. Feeling good again involves the removal of threats to self-worth.

The Conflict Sequence also describes the way people's focus and energy is concentrated as conflict progresses through stages.[4]

1.  In the **first stage**, the motivation is to respond to conflict in a way that is acceptable to everyone involved; the focus is on the self, the problem, and other people.

2.  The transition to the **second stage** is characterized by a narrowed focus and a concentration of energy on the self and the problem. Other people can be dropped from focus in the second stage, where the motivation is to resolve the conflict in a way that is acceptable to the individual in conflict.

3.  The transition to the **third stage** is characterized by a further concentration of energy and focus on the self. The problem can be dropped from focus in the third stage, where the motive is to protect, defend, or preserve the individual's sense of self.

Each Conflict Sequence can be understood as though it were assembled from different blocks, as shown in the Table 3.1. For example, the Conflict Sequence of R-G-B is:

● Stage 1 Red—wanting to rise to the challenge being offered.

● Stage 2 Green—wanting to escape from the other person or delay the issue.

● Stage 3 Blue—feeling driven to give up completely.

**Table 3.1** *Stages of Conflict by Color*[5]

| AREAS OF FOCUS | BLUE<br>*Accommodate* | RED<br>*Assert* | GREEN<br>*Analyze* |
|---|---|---|---|
| **STAGE 1: Responding** | | | |
| Self,<br>Problem,<br>Other | Wanting to accommodate the needs of others | Wanting to rise to the challenge being offered | Wanting to be prudently cautious |
| **STAGE 2: Narrowing** | | | |
| Self,<br>Problem,<br>~~Other~~ | Wanting to conditionally give in or defer to the other person | Wanting to prevail against the issue or other person | Wanting to escape from the other person or delay the issue |
| **STAGE 3: Defending** | | | |
| Self,<br>~~Problem,~~<br>~~Other~~ | Feeling driven to give up completely | Feeling driven to fight for one's life | Feeling driven to retreat completely |

When a Conflict Sequence has letters in brackets, it means that two colors of motivation are, for practical purposes, equal. For example, the Conflict Sequence of [RG]-B is:

- Stage 1 Red or Green—wanting to rise to the challenge being offered or wanting to be prudently cautious (or a combination of the two)

- Stage 2 Red or Green—wanting to prevail against the issue or person, or wanting to escape from the other person or delay the issue (or a combination of the two)

- Stage 3 Blue—feeling driven to give up completely.

## What are Conflict Filters?

Motives at the different stages of conflict give meaning to behavior, relationships, and situations. The Conflict Sequence can act as a filter through which life is perceived, interpreted, and understood. Filters stop some things and allow other things through. The Conflict Sequence filters and influences perception. Information deemed important is readily received, but information deemed irrelevant is actively or even subconsciously screened out of awareness.

Differences in conflict filters can help explain why two people can have entirely different memories of a shared experience or why one person believes there is a conflict when another person does not. Since behavior is a choice (even during conflict) and choices are limited to options that people perceive, the Conflict Sequence acts to constrain or expand the range of choices that people believe they have.

## What Doesn't the Conflict Sequence Do?

The Conflict Sequence does not indicate skills. However, people may want to develop skills in their first stage of conflict, so they can resolve conflict in the first stage and less frequently experience stages two and three. The Conflict Sequence is not an indicator of effectiveness; it describes what people want to do, not how well they do it. For example, people may want to be prudently cautious, but their caution during conflict may be exercised to such a degree that they do not actively engage in solving their problem.

The Conflict Sequence is not a certain forecast or guarantee of behavior. While it does help to understand, anticipate, and perhaps even predict the way people's motives change in conflict, people still have the ability to choose to act differently. Just because someone feels like fighting does not mean they will fight.

The Conflict Sequence and the numerical results that indicate it do not predict the speed with which people will enter conflict or go through the stages. Nor does it foretell the amount of time people will spend in the stages. It shows the order of the motivational changes that people experience as conflict intensifies. Other factors, such as the history of conflict in the relationship or the importance of the conflict trigger to people's senses of self-worth, may affect the speed or duration of conflict. A conflict can be resolved or left unresolved at any stage. If a conflict is resolved in Stage 1, there is no need to enter Stage 2 or Stage 3. A conflict does not need to go through all three stages in order to be resolved. Resolution can happen quickly, or it may take a long time.

## WHAT VARIABLES AFFECT CONFLICT?

There are 13 Conflict Sequences. While people with the same Conflict Sequence generally agree about why they do things during conflict, they may not necessarily agree about what to do in each situation. However, over time, patterns of common behavior can be observed.

Each Conflict Sequence covers a region of the SDI triangle that includes many possible SDI scores. Within each region, many differences are possible for scores and also for people. The Conflict Sequence scores show the order of changes in motivation.

Conflict can be a complex topic, with many variables affecting the way people approach it. If a conflict involves a core personal value or has some other strong tie to people's sense of self-worth, it's possible that they will be willing to engage the deeper stages of conflict. However, some conflicts involve less significant values and may be more readily released in earlier stages.

The way people express their motives in conflict may also be subject to situational or cultural expectations. For example, a person could feel similarly in two conflicts, one with a boss and one with a peer. It's possible that role expectations will influence the selection of different behaviors in these two situations, even though the feelings and motives are the same.

The history of conflict in a relationship may affect future conflicts. People who have repeatedly been unable to resolve conflict in Stage 1 may move quickly into Stage 2. This may cause it to appear that Stage 1 was skipped. However, when a current event is viewed as a continuation of a past conflict, and not as a new conflict, a different conclusion is possible. People may re-enter or re-engage a conflict at the point at which they previously left it; they go "in through the out door."

## WHAT'S NOT CONFLICT?

Conflict is different from opposition. It is possible to experience disagreements, differences of opinion, and uncertainty without also experiencing a threat to self-worth. These non-threatening differences are opposition and can be managed from the "going-well" state, rather than the conflict state.

The word conflict is often used to describe opposition or even negotiation. While it is tempting to connect the idea of a win-win solution to Stage 1 conflict, a win-lose solution to Stage 2 conflict, and a lose-lose solution to Stage

3 conflict, the Conflict Sequence describes changes in motivation, not the quality of outcomes. Winners and losers can be found in all stages of conflict. However, practical experience suggests that a win-win solution becomes less likely and more difficult to achieve as people get deeper into the stages of their Conflict Sequences.

## WHAT NEXT?

As you read the following sections, you may want to start with your own Conflict Sequence. Make notes in this book. When you find something useful, make it easy to find again. Remember that each section is written with a standard Conflict Sequence type in mind and that you will probably not agree with everything as presented, especially if your Conflict Sequence arrowhead is close to the border of another Conflict Sequence region on the triangle.

The Conflict Sequence is only half of the SDI. The MVS is the other half. These two halves are related to each other. We experience conflict only about things that are important us. The things that trigger conflict affect the way we experience conflict. Whatever gets us into conflict provides important clues about getting us out of conflict.

Don't stop with the Conflict Sequence. Understand more about your whole personality by considering how your Conflict Sequence connects to your MVS. Then do the same for other people. While the SDI is about you, it has the most value when you consider yourself in the context of your relationships.

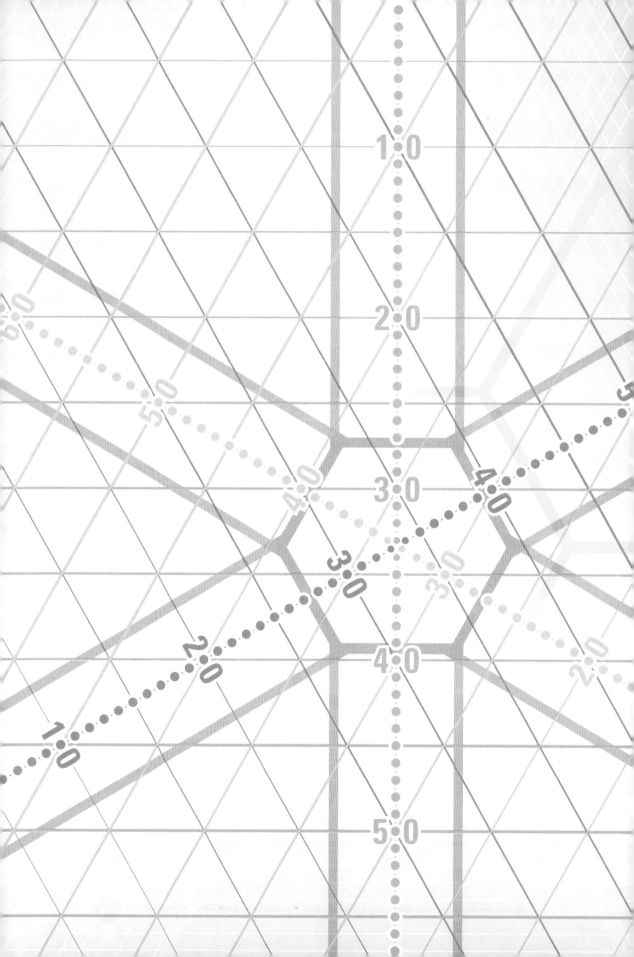

# B-R-G

## CONFLICT SEQUENCE

This Conflict Sequence describes people who want to keep peace and harmony. If that does not work, they want to take a stand for their rights. If that does not work, they may feel compelled to withdraw as a last resort.

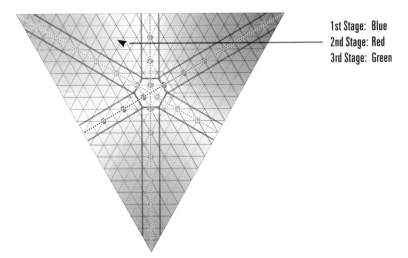

1st Stage:  Blue
2nd Stage:  Red
3rd Stage:  Green

This descriptive text is written with a Conflict Sequence arrowhead located about centrally in the Conflict Sequence region in mind. People whose arrowheads are close to the borders (within six points) of other Conflict Sequence regions may find that some text from the neighboring regions' descriptions is more accurate or useful.

While the following text describes the B-R-G Conflict Sequence, it should also be considered in light of the MVS of the person who has this Conflict Sequence. Since there are seven Motivational Value Systems, there are at least seven different ways to enter conflict and many different issues that can trigger conflict. These differences will affect the way people experience conflict and how they will resolve conflict. The first stage of this Conflict Sequence is Blue. People with a short arrow whose MVS is also Blue will experience a less noticeable transition from their MVS to the first stage of conflict than people whose MVS is a different color will.

## Stage 1 Blue Conflict

People in first stage Blue conflict are motivated by a desire to accommodate the needs of others. They want most to keep harmony and goodwill and may continue to appease the opposition in order to do so.

People in Stage 1 Blue tend to feel anxious and even agitated but reluctant to take action to identify the specific source of those feelings. They feel a strong sense of discomfort because conflict exists, and they want to explore why they feel as they do before they identify solutions for a potential problem.

In first stage Blue, people tend to make efforts to keep harmony and goodwill in the relationship. In order to achieve this, they may respond, when asked if anything is wrong with, "No, I'm fine; there's no problem." They often expect others to "just know" what is causing discomfort, in particular by interpreting their body language.

Productive first stage Blue conflict behaviors are typically used in an effort to minimize confrontation and to ensure that everyone is heard and that harmony is first pursued above individual resolution. They want to create an environment where those in conflict feel accommodated, so that resolution can occur in a non-threatening way.

When unproductive, people in first stage Blue may sacrifice their own rights or refuse to acknowledge that there is a problem. This may cause them to appear subservient or in denial. They may simply hope that the problem goes away on its own and avoid any potential confrontation.

### How People in Stage 1 Blue Can Borrow Behavior to Be More Effective

People who are experiencing the first stage of conflict may act as described previously. However, people may also borrow behavior or examine their perceptions during conflict in an effort to be more effective.

In Stage 1 Blue, people may be more effective if they:

- Consider the issue from as objective a vantage point as possible.
- Clearly state their personal priorities and boundaries.

- Determine whether they are able to accommodate and let go, or whether the accommodation will create an implied obligation on another person's part.

- Consider subtle signs of discomfort and what deeper issue they may represent.

## STAGE 2 RED CONFLICT

When initial efforts to maintain harmony and accommodate the needs of others are not effective at resolving conflict, people who then move into the second stage of Red carry a desire for peace and an awareness of others' needs with them.

In second stage Red (following Blue), people are frustrated and perhaps even hurt that they have not been heard. Their accommodation in Stage 1 may be missed by others or misperceived as compliance, or even agreement. Now, they feel totally justified in asserting their positions, often with energized words that may seem abrupt and hurtful to others involved in the conflict. At this point, the assertion is viewed as a justifiable use of force to win the battle. By standing up for their rights, they get others to understand the problem and return to a more harmonious state.

In second stage Red (following Blue), people may act more energetically, closing space and increasing volume in order to be heard. Feeling hurt by a lack of understanding, they actively assert their position. Their sense of being overlooked or unacknowledged results in a burst of emotion, which is intended to get others' attention and ensure that they are heard. By demanding a platform for expressing their concerns, they hope to restore the initial harmony.

People with a B-R-G Conflict Sequence generally work very hard in Stage 2 Red to prevent going to Stage 3 Green. They may continue to elevate the importance and urgency of the situation and the intensity of their reaction. They may believe that they are acting on their last chance to stay involved with a person or situation and that the fight, no matter how difficult, is better than walking away in Stage 3 Green.

## STAGE 3 GREEN CONFLICT

In the third stage of Green (following Blue and Red), people tend to abandon or insulate themselves from all feeling for the issue and the people involved. They tend to believe that their assertive and accommodating approaches to conflict have been met with a lack of cooperation or fair play and that no option remains except to disengage.

In the third stage of Green (following Blue and Red), people will typically withdraw and cut off contact in order to preserve whatever they can salvage from the situation. They may refuse to even talk about the past issue, because they think there is no remaining possibility of resolving it. If the conflict is severe, they may end the relationship and avoid all further interaction with the people involved.

### The Green Stage 3 Filter

Green is the third stage of conflict in the B-R-G sequence. While in first stage Blue and observing Green behavior in another person, some projection of the third stage experience onto the other is possible. Analytical behavior in others may be perceived as cold detachment without first considering the needs of others or engaging in problem-solving efforts.

## CONFLICT RESOLUTION

Conflict is resolved when the elements of opposition are addressed, and the people involved are able to return to feeling good about themselves again.

### The Path Back to the MVS from Stage 1 Blue

Each person has a path back from conflict to their MVS and feelings of self-worth. Even though many people may feel and act similarly in the first stage of conflict, there may be differences that are related to the MVS they are trying to return to. Conflict management efforts can be improved by keeping these differences in mind.

The path back to the MVS will be different for every person. Table 3.2 features some general illustrations of the path from Stage 1 Blue back to MVS.

**Figure 3.3** *Paths back to MVS from B-R-G*

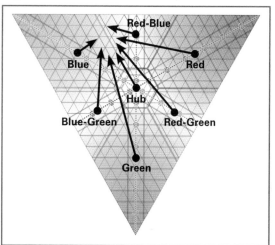

**Table 3.2** *Illustrations of the path back to MVS from Stage 1 Blue*

| | |
|---|---|
| Blue MVS | Restoring peace and reestablishing the value of the relationship |
| Red MVS | Smoothing things over and refocusing on results |
| Green MVS | Accepting the logic of others and clarifying underlying principles |
| Red-Blue MVS | Restoring, developing, and strengthening the relationship |
| Red-Green MVS | Letting go of small things to focus on the bigger strategy |
| Blue-Green MVS | Accommodating others and learning from mistakes |
| Hub MVS | Calming the situation so everyone can get reunited |

For more detailed information and ideas about resolving conflict with people who have this Conflict Sequence, also consult the "Productive Results of Conflict" sections in the chapters that describe the MVS of those people. No matter the MVS of the people in the conflict, there are some things that can help them transition out of Stage 1 Blue.

## HOW TO APPROACH PEOPLE WHILE THEY ARE IN STAGE 1 BLUE CONFLICT

- Affirm the relationship, and depersonalize the conflict.

- Be pleasant and genuine and invite responses.

- Be calm and non-confrontational.

- Allow the person to lead the conversation toward the point they really want to make.

- Listen, and ask more than once if needed.

- Respect the person's request for time and space.

## THINGS TO AVOID WHEN APPROACHING PEOPLE WHILE THEY ARE IN STAGE 1 BLUE CONFLICT

- Focusing on resolving the conflict quickly or exclusively on the facts.

- Being aggressive toward the person or confronting them in public.

- Being sarcastic or patronizing.

# B-G-R
## CONFLICT SEQUENCE

This Conflict Sequence describes people who want to keep harmony and goodwill. If that does not work, they want to disengage and save what they can. If that does not work, they may feel compelled to fight, possibly in an explosive manner.

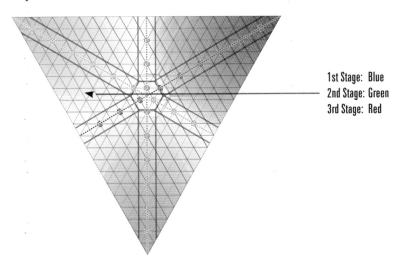

1st Stage: Blue
2nd Stage: Green
3rd Stage: Red

This descriptive text is written with a Conflict Sequence arrowhead located about centrally in the Conflict Sequence region in mind. People whose arrowheads are close to the borders (within six points) of other Conflict Sequence regions may find that some text from the neighboring regions' descriptions is more accurate or useful.

While the following text describes the B-G-R Conflict Sequence, it should also be considered in light of the MVS of the person who has this Conflict Sequence. Since there are seven Motivational Value Systems, there are at least seven different ways to enter conflict and many different issues that can trigger conflict. These differences will affect the way people experience conflict and how they will resolve conflict. The first stage of this Conflict Sequence is Blue. People with a short arrow whose MVS is also Blue, will experience a less noticeable transition from their MVS to the first stage of conflict than people whose MVS is a different color will.

## STAGE 1 BLUE CONFLICT

People in first stage Blue conflict are motivated by a desire to accommodate the needs of others. They want most to keep harmony and goodwill and may continue to appease the opposition in order to do so.

People in Stage 1 Blue tend to feel anxious and even agitated but reluctant to take action to identify the specific source of those feelings. They feel a strong sense of discomfort because conflict exists, and they want to explore why they feel as they do before they identify solutions for a potential problem.

In first stage Blue, people tend to make efforts to keep harmony and goodwill in the relationship. In order to achieve this, they may respond, when asked if anything is wrong with, "No, I'm fine; there's no problem." They often expect others to "just know" what is causing discomfort, in particular by interpreting their body language.

Productive first stage Blue conflict behaviors are typically used in an effort to minimize confrontation and to ensure that everyone is heard and that harmony is first pursued above individual resolution. They want to create an environment where those in conflict feel accommodated, so that resolution can occur in a non-threatening way.

When unproductive, people in first stage Blue may sacrifice their own rights or refuse to acknowledge that there is a problem. This may cause them to appear subservient or in denial. They may simply hope that the problem goes away on its own and avoid any potential confrontation.

### How People in Stage 1 Blue Can Borrow Behavior to Be More Effective

People who are experiencing the first stage of conflict may act as described previously. However, people may also borrow behavior or examine their perceptions during conflict in an effort to be more effective.

In Stage 1 Blue, people may be more effective if they:

- Consider the issue from as objective a vantage point as possible.
- Clearly state their personal priorities and boundaries.

- Determine whether they are able to accommodate and let go or whether the accommodation will create an implied obligation on another person's part.

- Consider subtle signs of discomfort and what deeper issue they may represent.

## STAGE 2 GREEN CONFLICT

When initial efforts to maintain harmony and accommodate the needs of others are not effective at resolving the conflict, people who then move into the second stage of Green (following Blue) carry a desire for peace and an awareness of others' needs with them.

In second stage Green (following Blue), people feel unable to restore harmony and goodwill. In fact, it is possible that the efforts to restore that goodwill in Stage 1 may be missed or misperceived as compliance or even agreement. Therefore, they try to disengage and save what can be saved. They may feel the need to become quiet and withdrawn as they try to think through a solution that regains the harmony that is lost. They want to come up with "just the right words" to resolve the confrontation.

In second stage Green (following Blue), people may become quiet and distance themselves from others. They consider and reconsider their position, gathering information to give their position strength. At this point, they try an objective approach to the situation, stepping back from their feelings and their anxiety about those feelings. They focus on solving whatever can be solved, attempting to understand and make adjustments in the conflict, while always thinking about how to restore harmony and goodwill.

People with a B-G-R Conflict Sequence generally work very hard in Stage 2 Green to prevent going to Stage 3 Red. They may continue to collect information about the situation and the people involved in an effort to find some sort of rational solution to the problem. They may hold their position and wait, even for extended periods of time, believing that waiting is better than allowing themselves to slip into the potentially explosive situation of Stage 3 Red.

## STAGE 3 RED CONFLICT

In the third stage of Red (following Blue and Green), people tend to feel intensely angry, energized, and potentially out of control, demanding an "all or nothing" solution. They tend to feel that all of their efforts to resolve the issue logically and without confrontation have failed. They feel that the desired outcome must be forcibly taken or forcibly denied to the other person, regardless of cost.

In the third stage of Red (following Blue and Green), people will typically challenge others or fight others, potentially in an explosive manner. They may say that they no longer care what other people think or want, forcibly implementing whatever they originally thought was the best solution. If the conflict is severe, the relationship may be irreparably damaged by the harshness of personal attacks or by the negative reactions of people who view this third stage red behavior as overblown and uncalled for.

### The Red Stage 3 Filter

Red is the third stage of conflict in the B-G-R sequence. While in first stage Blue and observing Red behavior in another person, some projection of the third stage experience on the other is possible. Assertive behavior of others may be perceived as angry overreaction without first taking the time to consider the needs of others or the facts of the situation.

## CONFLICT RESOLUTION

Conflict is resolved when the elements of opposition are addressed and the people involved are able to return to feeling good about themselves again.

### The Path Back to the MVS from Stage 1 Blue

Each person has a path back from conflict to their MVS and feelings of self-worth. Even though many people may feel and act similarly in the first stage of conflict, there may be differences that are related to the MVS they are trying to return to. Conflict management efforts can be improved by keeping these differences in mind.

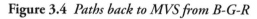

**Figure 3.4 _Paths back to MVS from B-G-R_**

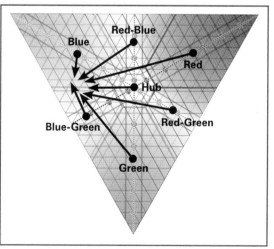

The path back to the MVS will be different for every person. Table 3.3 features some general illustrations of the path from Stage 1 Blue back to MVS.

**Table 3.3** *Illustrations of the path back to MVS from Stage 1 Blue*

| | |
|---|---|
| Blue MVS | Restoring peace and reestablishing the value of the relationship |
| Red MVS | Smoothing things over and refocusing on results |
| Green MVS | Accepting the logic of others and clarifying underlying principles |
| Red-Blue MVS | Restoring, developing, and strengthening the relationship |
| Red-Green MVS | Letting go of small things to focus on the bigger strategy |
| Blue-Green MVS | Accommodating others and learning from mistakes |
| Hub MVS | Calming the situation so everyone can get reunited |

For more detailed information and ideas about resolving conflict with people who have this Conflict Sequence, also consult the "Productive Results of Conflict" sections in the chapters that describe the MVS of those people. No matter the MVS of people in the conflict, there are some things that can help them transition out of Stage 1 Blue.

## HOW TO APPROACH PEOPLE WHILE THEY ARE IN STAGE 1 BLUE CONFLICT

● Affirm the relationship, and depersonalize the conflict.

● Be pleasant and genuine, and invite responses.

● Be calm and non-confrontational.

● Allow the person to lead the conversation toward the point they really want to make.

- Listen, ask more than once if needed.

- Respect the person's request for time and space.

## THINGS TO AVOID WHEN APPROACHING PEOPLE WHILE THEY ARE IN STAGE 1 BLUE CONFLICT

- Focusing on resolving the conflict quickly or exclusively on the facts.

- Being aggressive toward the person or confronting them in public.

- Being sarcastic or patronizing.

# B-[RG]

## CONFLICT SEQUENCE

This Conflict Sequence describes people who want to keep harmony and accommodate the opposition. If that does not work, they want to make a choice based on what's best for everyone: to rely on logic and principle or to employ assertive strategies to prevent defeat.

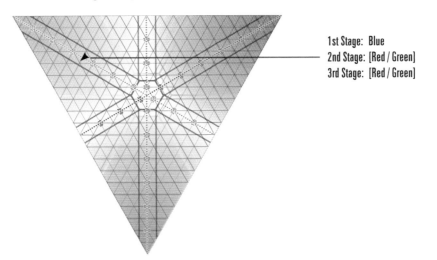

1st Stage: Blue
2nd Stage: [Red / Green]
3rd Stage: [Red / Green]

This descriptive text is written with a Conflict Sequence arrowhead located centrally in the Conflict Sequence region in mind. People whose arrowheads are close to the borders (within six points) of other Conflict Sequence regions may find that some text from the neighboring regions' descriptions is more accurate or useful.

While the following text describes the B-[RG] Conflict Sequence, it should also be considered in light of the MVS of the person who has this Conflict Sequence. Since there are seven Motivational Value Systems, there are at least seven different ways to enter conflict and many different issues that can trigger conflict.

These differences will affect the way people experience conflict and how they will resolve conflict. The first stage of this Conflict Sequence is Blue. People with a short arrow whose MVS is also Blue, will experience a less noticeable transition from their MVS to the first stage of conflict than people whose MVS is a different color will.

## STAGE 1 BLUE CONFLICT

People in first stage Blue conflict are motivated by a desire to accommodate the needs of others. They want most to keep harmony and goodwill and may continue to appease the opposition in order to do so.

People in Stage 1 Blue tend to feel anxious and even agitated but reluctant to take action to identify the specific source of those feelings. They feel a strong sense of discomfort because conflict exists, and they want to explore why they feel as they do before they identify solutions for a potential problem.

In first stage Blue, people tend to make efforts to keep harmony and goodwill in the relationship. In order to achieve this, they may respond, when asked if anything is wrong with, "No, I'm fine; there's no problem." They often expect others to "just know" what is causing discomfort, in particular by interpreting their body language.

Productive first stage Blue conflict behaviors are typically used in an effort to minimize confrontation and to ensure that everyone is heard and that harmony is first pursued above individual resolution. They want to create an environment where those in conflict feel accommodated, so that resolution can occur in a non-threatening way.

When unproductive, people in first stage Blue may sacrifice their own rights or refuse to acknowledge that there is a problem. This may cause them to appear subservient or in denial. They may simply hope that the problem goes away on its own and avoid any potential confrontation.

### How People in Stage 1 Blue Can Borrow Behavior to Be More Effective

People who are experiencing the first stage of conflict may act as described previously. However, people may also borrow behavior or examine their perceptions during conflict in an effort to be more effective.

In Stage 1 Blue, people may be more effective if they:

- Consider the issue from as objective a vantage point as possible.

- Clearly state their personal priorities and boundaries.

- Determine whether they are able to accommodate and let go or whether the accommodation will create an implied obligation on another person's part.

- Consider subtle signs of discomfort and what deeper issue they may represent.

## STAGE 2 BLENDED RED & GREEN CONFLICT

When initial efforts to maintain harmony and accommodate the needs of others are not effective at resolving the conflict, people who then move into the second stage of Red/Green carry their desire for peace and awareness of others' needs with them.

People in this blended second and third stage may take different approaches, based on their perception of the situation. They may go to Red followed by Green if the results are more important than the principles involved or to Green followed by Red if the principles are more important than the results. In these cases, conflict can be understood more fully by referring to the B-R-G and B-G-R pages. It is also possible that the Red and Green conflict stages will be combined for a blended conflict experience.

When Red and Green are blended in Stages 2 and 3, people are done with accommodating others to solve the problem. Pressed far enough, they now feel the need to fall back on logical and assertive strategies to preserve their integrity and to prevent unfair accommodation of others. These people have a strong desire to find an effective strategy, which they are willing to implement forcefully if necessary.

Once a strategy has been identified, they want to drive their agenda and decisively overcome objections. If a rational end to the conflict cannot be achieved quickly, they may begin to formulate worst-case scenarios or ultimatums, which may be acted on from the third stage.

## STAGE 3 BLENDED RED & GREEN CONFLICT

While Red and Green are blended in Stages 2 and 3, people will experience an internal difference between these stages. Stage 2 is characterized by a focus on the self and the problem, and Stage 3 is focused on the self. Therefore, the Stage 3 experience of Red/Green is a more intense and self-focused version of the Stage 2 experience. If a person concentrated on an assertive, Red approach in Stage 2, their third stage is likely to be the detached withdrawal typical of Stage 3 Green. If they concentrated on the analytical, Green approach to Stage 2, their third stage is likely to be the explosive fighting typical of Stage 3 Red.

### The Blended Red & Green Stage 3 Filter

Red/Green is the blended second and third stage of conflict in the B-[RG] sequence. While in first stage Blue and observing Red-Green behavior in another person, some projection of the second or third stage experience on the other is possible. Strategic behavior of others may be perceived as manipulative and without regard for the needs of others.

## CONFLICT RESOLUTION

Conflict is resolved when the elements of opposition are addressed, and the people involved are able to return to feeling good about themselves again.

### The Path Back to the MVS from Stage 1 Blue

Each person has a path back from conflict to their MVS and feelings of self-worth. Even though many people may feel and act similarly in the first stage of conflict, there may be differences that are related to the MVS they are trying to return to. Conflict management efforts can be improved by keeping these differences in mind.

The path back to the MVS will be different for every person. Table 3.4 features some general illustrations of the path from Stage 1 Blue back to MVS.

**Figure 3.5** *Paths back to MVS from B-[RG]*

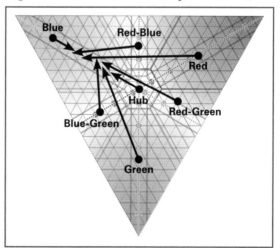

**Table 3.4** *Illustrations of the path back to MVS from Stage 1 Blue*

| | |
|---|---|
| Blue MVS | Restoring peace and reestablishing the value of the relationship |
| Red MVS | Smoothing things over and refocusing on results |
| Green MVS | Accepting the logic of others and clarifying underlying principles |
| Red-Blue MVS | Restoring, developing, and strengthening the relationship |
| Red-Green MVS | Letting go of small things to focus on the bigger strategy |
| Blue-Green MVS | Accommodating others and learning from mistakes |
| Hub MVS | Calming the situation so everyone can get reunited |

For more detailed information and ideas about resolving conflict with people who have this Conflict Sequence, also consult the "Productive Results of Conflict" sections in the chapters that describe the MVS of those people. No matter the MVS of people in the conflict, there are some things that can help them transition out of Stage 1 Blue.

## HOW TO APPROACH PEOPLE WHILE THEY ARE IN STAGE 1 BLUE CONFLICT

- Affirm the relationship and depersonalize the conflict.

- Be pleasant and genuine, and invite responses.

- Be calm and non-confrontational.

- Allow the person lead to the conversation toward the point they really want to make.

- Listen, and ask more than once if needed.

- Respect the person's request for time and space.

## Things to Avoid When Approaching People While They Are in Stage 1 Blue Conflict

- Focusing on resolving the conflict quickly or exclusively on the facts.

- Being aggressive toward the person or confronting them in public.

- Being sarcastic or patronizing.

# R-B-G

## CONFLICT SEQUENCE

This sequence describes people who want to challenge conflict directly. If that does not work, they want to restore or preserve harmony. If that does not work, they may want to withdraw from the situation or end the relationship.

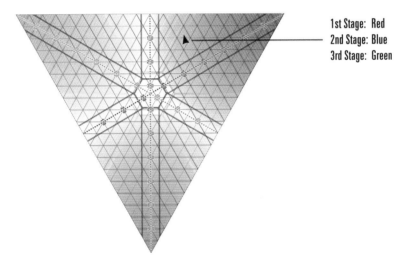

1st Stage: Red
2nd Stage: Blue
3rd Stage: Green

This descriptive text is written with a Conflict Sequence arrowhead located centrally in the Conflict Sequence region in mind. People whose arrowheads are close to the borders (within six points) of other Conflict Sequence regions may find that some text from the neighboring regions' descriptions is more accurate or useful.

While the following text describes the R-B-G Conflict Sequence, it should also be considered in light of the MVS of the person who has this Conflict Sequence. Since there are seven Motivational Value Systems, there are at least seven different ways to enter conflict and many different issues that can trigger conflict. These differences will affect the way people experience conflict and how they will resolve conflict. The first stage of this Conflict Sequence is Red. People with a short arrow whose MVS is also Red, will experience a less noticeable transition from their MVS to the first stage of conflict than people whose MVS is a different color will.

## STAGE 1 RED CONFLICT

People in first stage Red conflict are motivated by the desire to rise to the challenge being offered. They tend to meet conflict head-on, with strong self-assertion and challenge to the opposition.

In first stage Red, people tend to feel energized and have a sense of certainty about what needs to be done. They feel a sense of urgency about solving the conflict and expect others to reflect that urgency back to them by taking action. If they do not sense that others feel a similar sense of urgency, they may press others for an immediate response.

In Stage 1 Red, people tend to come out competing to prevail over the opposition. They are quick to assert their rights and to argue persuasively for them in the moment. They press for an immediate resolution of the conflict. Their intensity may cause others to back away from the interaction, unintentionally delaying the engagement that people in first stage Red want.

Productive first stage Red conflict behaviors are typically targeted directly at the problem and the people involved. First stage Reds want to engage the issue as quickly as possible. The desire is to solve the problem rapidly and with the best possible result. Their assertive behaviors are intended to provide a quick answer to the opposition and an expedient response to the conflict issue.

When unproductive, people in first stage Red may push too hard or act too quickly. This may cause them to appear argumentative, angry, pushy, or rash. They may become so focused on the need for action and the urgency of the situation that they are not open to others' ideas.

### How People in Stage 1 Red Can Borrow Behavior to Be More Effective

People who are experiencing the first stage of conflict may act as described previously. However, people may also borrow behavior or examine their perceptions during conflict in an effort to be more effective.

In Stage 1 Red, people may be more effective if they:

- Take time to consider the issue from as neutral a vantage point as possible.

- Listen carefully to the facts and feelings expressed by others.

- Determine whether there are alternative approaches to the one that seems most obvious in the moment.

- Consider the implications of doing nothing or waiting.

## STAGE 2 BLUE CONFLICT

When initial actions to meet the challenge decisively are not effective at resolving the conflict, people who then move into the second stage of Blue (following Red) carry their passion for the issue and their desire for results with them.

In second stage Blue (following Red), people may feel they have pushed too hard or overreacted and now want to restore harmony or repair any unintentional damage they may have done. This second stage is about putting aside their ambitions in order to get other people back on board with the vision. They may also feel tired of the struggle and just want people to get along, even if the results are slightly less than optimal.

In second stage Blue (following Red), people want to let go of the struggle. They may still hold a strong position but no longer want to talk about it. If they are pushed further at this point, they may throw up their hands and respond with, "OK, fine. Whatever." Although this appears to be a sort of surrender, it is conditional, and they may still be upset. They may be back to re-engage after they have recovered their energy for the issue.

People with a R-B-G Conflict Sequence generally work very hard in Stage 2 Blue to prevent going to Stage 3 Green. They may continue to appease others through accommodation or apology if they believe they overreacted in Stage 1 Red. They may put aside their own wishes, believing that sacrifice allows them to stay engaged and is better than walking away in Stage 3 Green.

## STAGE 3 GREEN CONFLICT

In the third stage of Green (following Red and Blue), people tend to abandon or insulate themselves from feelings for the issue and the people involved. They tend to believe that their assertive and accommodating approaches to conflict have been met with a lack of cooperation or fair play and that no option remains except to disengage.

In the third stage of Green (following Red and Blue) people will typically withdraw and cut off contact in order to preserve whatever they can salvage from the situation. They may refuse to even talk about the past issue because they think there is no remaining possibility of resolving it. If the conflict is severe, they may end the relationship and avoid all further interaction with the people involved.

### The Green Stage 3 Filter

Green is the third stage of conflict in the R-B-G sequence. When in first stage Red and observing Green behavior in another person, some projection of the third stage experience on the other is possible. Analytical behavior of others may be perceived as uncommitted detachment without first taking a stand, sensing the urgency of the situation, or engaging in problem-solving efforts.

## CONFLICT RESOLUTION

Conflict is resolved when the elements of opposition are addressed and the people involved are able to return to feeling good about themselves again.

### The Path Back to the MVS from Stage 1 Red

Each person has a path back from conflict to their MVS and feelings of self-worth. Even though many people may feel and act similarly in the first stage of conflict, there may be differences that are related to the MVS they are trying to return to. Conflict management efforts can be improved by keeping these differences in mind.

**Figure 3.6** *Paths back to MVS from R-B-G*

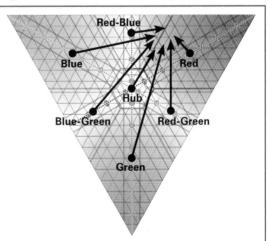

The path back to the MVS will be different for every person. Table 3.5 features some general illustrations of the path from Stage 1 Red back to MVS.

**Table 3.5** *Illustrations of the path back to MVS from Stage 1 Red*

| | |
|---|---|
| Blue MVS | Taking immediate action that benefits others |
| Red MVS | Meeting the challenge and refocusing on the results |
| Green MVS | Acting with urgency to restore order and logic |
| Red-Blue MVS | Challenging others to grow by overcoming obstacles |
| Red-Green MVS | Proving the validity of a strategy through decisive action |
| Blue-Green MVS | Fighting for principles to restore fairness and self-sufficiency |
| Hub MVS | Choosing the least constraining option and acting swiftly on it |

For more detailed information and ideas about resolving conflict with people who have this Conflict Sequence, also consult the "Productive Results of Conflict" sections in the chapters that describe the MVS of those people. No matter the MVS of people in the conflict, there are some things that can help them transition out of Stage 1 Red.

## How to Approach People While They Are in Stage 1 Red Conflict

- Listen and acknowledge their position, then respond directly, openly, and honestly.

- Take a confident stand, discussing your point of view and raising relevant issues.

- Be prepared for a robust exchange of views.

- Be purposeful and direct.

- Focus on resolving the issue and taking action.

- Be energetic and passionate, demonstrating an understanding of the issue's importance.

## THINGS TO AVOID WHEN APPROACHING PEOPLE WHILE THEY ARE IN STAGE 1 RED CONFLICT

- Focusing on minor details or emotional issues.

- Trivializing, walking away, or giving in without reason.

- Telling them they are angry or telling them to "calm down."

# R-G-B
## CONFLICT SEQUENCE

This Conflict Sequence describes people who want to prevail through competition. If that does not work, they want to use logic, reason, and rules. If that does not work, they may feel compelled to surrender as a last resort.

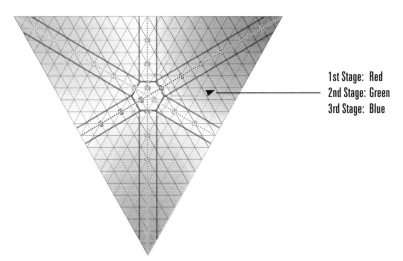

1st Stage: Red
2nd Stage: Green
3rd Stage: Blue

This descriptive text is written with a Conflict Sequence arrowhead located centrally in the Conflict Sequence region in mind. People whose arrowheads are close to the borders (within six points) of other Conflict Sequence regions may find that some text from the neighboring regions' descriptions is more accurate or useful.

While the following text describes the R-G-B Conflict Sequence, it should also be considered in light of the MVS of the person who has this Conflict Sequence. Since there are seven Motivational Value Systems, there are at least seven different ways to enter conflict and many different issues that can trigger conflict. These differences will affect the way people experience conflict and how they will resolve conflict. The first stage of this Conflict Sequence is Red.

People with a short arrow whose MVS is also Red will experience and less noticeable transition from their MVS to the first stage of conflict than people whose MVS is a different color will.

## STAGE 1 RED CONFLICT

People in first stage Red conflict are motivated by the desire to rise to the challenge being offered. They tend to meet conflict head-on, with strong self-assertion a nd challenge to the opposition.

In first stage Red, people tend to feel energized and have a sense of certainty about what needs to be done. They feel a sense of urgency about solving the conflict and expect others to reflect that urgency back to them by taking action. If they do not sense that others feel a similar sense of urgency, they may press others for an immediate response.

In Stage 1 Red, people tend to come out competing to prevail over the opposition. They are quick to assert their rights and to argue persuasively for them in the moment. They press for an immediate resolution of the conflict. Their intensity may cause others to back away from the interaction, unintentionally delaying the engagement that people in first stage Red want.

Productive first stage Red conflict behaviors are typically targeted directly at the problem and the people involved. First stage Reds want to engage the issue as quickly as possible. The desire is to solve the problem rapidly and with the best possible result. Their assertive behaviors are intended to provide a quick answer to the opposition and an expedient response to the conflict issue.

When unproductive, people in first stage Red may push too hard or act too quickly. This may cause them to appear argumentative, angry, pushy, or rash. They may become so focused on the need for action and the urgency of the situation that they are not open to others' ideas.

### How People in Stage 1 Red Can Borrow Behavior to Be More Effective

People who are experiencing the first stage of conflict may act as described previously. However, people may also borrow behavior or examine their perceptions during conflict in an effort to be more effective.

In Stage 1 Red, people may be more effective if they:

- Take time to consider the issue from as neutral a vantage point as possible.

- Listen carefully to the facts and feelings expressed by others.

- Determine whether there are alternative approaches to the one that seems most obvious in the moment.

- Consider the implications of doing nothing or waiting.

## STAGE 2 GREEN CONFLICT

When initial actions to meet the challenge decisively are not effective at resolving the conflict, people who then move into the second stage of Green (following Red) carry their passion for the issue and their desire for results with them.

In second stage Green (following Red), people feel that since competition and challenge did not produce a quick and desirable solution, they now need to fall back on analysis and logic. They may still feel a strong sense of rightness about their prior position, but they are willing to look at facts that will either support or challenge their initial position. They want some time and space away from others in order to think about how they can strengthen or improve their plan.

In second stage Green (following Red), people step back, taking the time to logically and thoughtfully assess the situation. Setting aside the desire to win in the moment, they analyze the situation and people's roles in it in order to identify a strategy to resolve the conflict more efficiently.

People with an R-G-B Conflict Sequence generally work very hard in Stage 2 Green to prevent going to Stage 3 Blue. They may continue to collect information to support or challenge positions held by themselves and others. They may become rigid and inflexible, believing that they are building a case that, if lost, cannot be salvaged if they are forced into a Stage 3 Blue experience.

## STAGE 3 BLUE CONFLICT

In the third stage of Blue (following Red and Green), people tend to feel completely defeated, not by others, but by the inability to find and implement a solution. They tend to feel that all of their efforts to resolve the issue logically and forcefully have failed, and all that remains is to give up on the issue and figure out how to live with the pain of defeat.

In the third stage of Blue (following Red and Green), people will typically end association with the issue and the people. They may say that they no longer care about the conflict or the impact on the people involved. If the conflict is severe, the relationship may be irreparably damaged by the inability to become emotionally involved again.

### The Blue Stage 3 Filter

Blue is the third stage of conflict in the R-G-B sequence. When in first stage Red and observing Blue behavior in another person, some projection of the third stage experience onto the other is possible. Accommodating behavior of others may be perceived as weakness, giving up, or lack of commitment, without any attempt to stand up for themselves or assert their rights.

## CONFLICT RESOLUTION

Conflict is resolved when the elements of opposition are addressed and the people involved are able to return to feeling good about themselves again.

### The Path Back to the MVS from Stage 1 Red

Each person has a path back from conflict to their MVS and feelings of self-worth. Even though many people may feel and act similarly in the first stage of conflict, there may be differences that are related to the MVS they are trying to return to. Conflict management efforts can be improved by keeping these differences in mind.

**Figure 3.7** *Paths back to MVS from R-G-B*

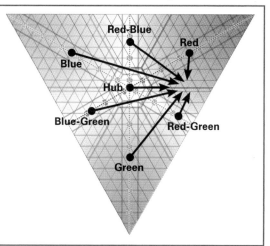

The path back to the MVS will be different for every person. Table 3.6 features some general illustrations of the path from Stage 1 Red back to MVS.

**Table 3.6** *Illustrations of the path back to MVS from Stage 1 Red*

| | |
|---|---|
| Blue MVS | Taking immediate action that benefits others |
| Red MVS | Meeting the challenge and refocusing on the results |
| Green MVS | Acting with urgency to restore order and logic |
| Red-Blue MVS | Challenging others to grow by overcoming obstacles |
| Red-Green MVS | Proving the validity of a strategy through decisive action |
| Blue-Green MVS | Fighting for principles to restore fairness and self-sufficiency |
| Hub MVS | Choosing the least constraining option and acting swiftly on it |

For more detailed information and ideas about resolving conflict with people who have this Conflict Sequence, also consult the "Productive Results of Conflict" sections in the chapters that describe the MVS of those people. No matter the MVS of people in the conflict, there are some things that can help them transition out of Stage 1 Red.

## How to Approach People While They Are in Stage 1 Red Conflict

- Listen and acknowledge their position, then respond directly, openly, and honestly.

- Take a confident stand, discussing your point of view and raising relevant issues.

- Be prepared for a robust exchange of views.

- Be purposeful and direct.

- Focus on resolving the issue and taking action.

- Be energetic and passionate, demonstrating an understanding of the issue's importance.

## THINGS TO AVOID WHEN APPROACHING PEOPLE WHILE THEY ARE IN STAGE 1 RED CONFLICT

- Focusing on minor details or emotional issues.

- Trivializing, walking away, or giving in without reason.

- Telling them they are angry or telling them to "calm down."

# R-[BG]
## CONFLICT SEQUENCE

This Conflict Sequence describes people who want to assert their rights and win. If that does not work, they want to make a choice, depending on what's better in the situation: to give in with conditions or to disengage and save what they can.

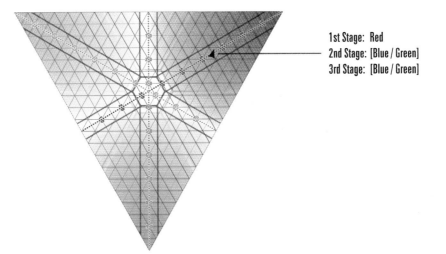

1st Stage: Red
2nd Stage: [Blue / Green]
3rd Stage: [Blue / Green]

This descriptive text is written with a Conflict Sequence arrowhead located centrally in the Conflict Sequence region in mind. People whose arrowheads are close to the borders (within six points) of other Conflict Sequence regions may find that some text from the neighboring regions' descriptions is more accurate or useful.

While the following text describes the R-[BG] Conflict Sequence, it should also be considered in light of the MVS of the person who has this Conflict Sequence. Since there are seven Motivational Value Systems, there are at least seven different ways to enter conflict, and many different issues that can trigger conflict. These differences will affect the way people experience conflict and how they will resolve conflict. The first stage of this Conflict Sequence is Red.

People with a short arrow whose MVS is also Red will experience a less noticeable transition from their MVS to the first stage of conflict than people whose MVS is a different color will.

## STAGE 1 RED CONFLICT

People in first stage Red conflict are motivated by the desire to rise to the challenge being offered. They tend to meet conflict head-on, with strong self-assertion and challenge to the opposition.

In first stage Red, people tend to feel energized and have a sense of certainty about what needs to be done. They feel a sense of urgency about solving the conflict and expect others to reflect that urgency back to them by taking action. If they do not sense that others feel a similar sense of urgency, they may press others for an immediate response.

In Stage 1 Red, people tend to come out competing to prevail over the opposition. They are quick to assert their rights and to argue persuasively for them in the moment. They press for an immediate resolution of the conflict. Their intensity may cause others to back away from the interaction, unintentionally delaying the engagement that people in first stage Red want.

Productive first stage Red conflict behaviors are typically targeted directly at the problem and the people involved. First stage Reds want to engage the issue as quickly as possible. The desire is to solve the problem rapidly and with the best possible result. Their assertive behaviors are intended to provide a quick answer to the opposition and an expedient response to the conflict issue.

When unproductive, people in first stage Red may push too hard or act too quickly. This may cause them to appear argumentative, angry, pushy, or rash. They may become so focused on the need for action and the urgency of the situation that they are not open to others' ideas.

## HOW PEOPLE IN STAGE 1 RED CAN BORROW BEHAVIOR TO BE MORE EFFECTIVE

People who are experiencing the first stage of conflict may act as described previously. However, people may also borrow behavior or examine their perceptions during conflict in an effort to be more effective.

In Stage 1 Red, people may be more effective if they:

- Take time to consider the issue from as neutral a vantage point as possible.
- Listen carefully to the facts and feelings expressed by others.
- Determine whether there are alternative approaches to the one that seems most obvious in the moment.
- Consider the implications of doing nothing or waiting.

## STAGE 2 BLEND OF BLUE & GREEN CONFLICT

When initial actions to meet the challenge decisively are not effective at resolving the conflict, people who then move into the second stage of Blue/Green carry their passion for the issue and their desire for results with them.

People in this blended second and third stage may take different approaches, based on their perception of the situation. They may go to Blue followed by Green if the relationship is more important than the principles involved or to Green followed by Blue if the principles are more important than the relationship. In these cases, conflict can be understood more fully by referring to the R-B-G and R-G-B pages. It is also possible that the Blue and Green conflict stages will be combined for a blended conflict experience.

When Blue and Green are blended in Stages 2 and 3 (following Red), people feel that they have pushed the issue hard enough and want to back off a bit. They want to take some time to reconsider the issue and their role in it. Because their direct engagement did not result in resolution, they may give in temporarily, apologizing for their assertiveness, conceding to their opposition, or doing some additional research about the conflict.

Ideally, they will be able to reconcile their differences and solve the problem. If they cannot and they do not openly concede or apologize, they may instead choose to wait the issue out, hoping that circumstances will change.

## STAGE 3 BLEND OF BLUE & GREEN CONFLICT

While Blue and Green are blended in Stages 2 and 3, people will experience an internal difference between these stages. Stage 2 is characterized by a focus on the self and the problem, and Stage 3 is focused on the self. Therefore, the Stage 3 experience of Blue/Green is a more intense and self-focused version of the Stage 2 experience. If a person concentrated on a conditionally accommodating, Blue approach in Stage 2, their third stage is likely to be the detached withdrawal typical of Stage 3 Green. If they concentrated on the analytical, Green approach to Stage 2, their third stage is likely to be the painful defeat or surrender typical of Stage 3 Blue.

### The Blend of Blue & Green Stage 3 Filter

(Blue-Green) is the blended second and third stage of conflict in the R-[BG] sequence. When in first stage Red and observing Blue-Green behavior in another person, some projection of the second or third stage experience on the other is possible. The cautious behavior of others may be perceived as passive-aggressive and without concern for the issue at hand.

## CONFLICT RESOLUTION

Conflict is resolved when the elements of opposition are addressed and the people involved are able to return to feeling good about themselves again.

### The Path Back to the MVS from Stage 1 Red

Each person has a path back from conflict to their MVS and feelings of self-worth. Even though many people may feel and act similarly in the first stage of conflict, there may be differences that are related to the MVS they are trying to return to. Conflict management efforts can be improved by keeping these differences in mind.

The path back to the MVS will be different for every person. Table 3.7 features some general illustrations of the path from Stage 1 Red back to MVS.

**Figure 3.8** *Paths back to MVS from R-[BG]*

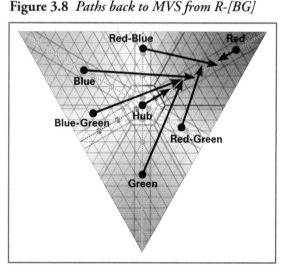

**Table 3.7** *Illustrations of the path back to MVS from Stage 1 Red*

| | |
|---|---|
| Blue MVS | Taking immediate action that benefits others |
| Red MVS | Meeting the challenge and refocusing on the results |
| Green MVS | Acting with urgency to restore order and logic |
| Red-Blue MVS | Challenging others to grow by overcoming obstacles |
| Red-Green MVS | Proving the validity of a strategy through decisive action |
| Blue-Green MVS | Fighting for principles to restore fairness and self-sufficiency |
| Hub MVS | Choosing the least constraining option and acting swiftly on it |

For more detailed information and ideas about resolving conflict with people who have this Conflict Sequence, also consult the "Productive Results of Conflict" sections in the chapters that describe the MVS of those people. No matter the MVS of people in the conflict, there are some things that can help them transition out of Stage 1 Red.

## How to Approach People While They Are in Stage 1 Red Conflict

- Listen and acknowledge their position, then respond directly, openly, and honestly.

- Take a confident stand, discussing your point of view and raising relevant issues.

- Be prepared for a robust exchange of views.

- Be purposeful and direct.

- Focus on resolving the issue and taking action.

- Be energetic and passionate, demonstrating an understanding of the issue's importance.

## Things to Avoid When Approaching People While They Are in Stage 1 Red Conflict

- Focusing on minor details or emotional issues.

- Trivializing, walking away, or giving in without reason.

- Telling them they are angry or telling them to "calm down."

# G-B-R

## CONFLICT SEQUENCE

This Conflict Sequence describes people who want to carefully examine the situation. If that does not work, they want to defer to other people in the interest of harmony. If that does not work, they may feel compelled to fight, possibly in an explosive manner.

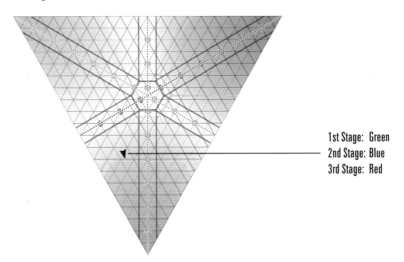

1st Stage: Green
2nd Stage: Blue
3rd Stage: Red

This descriptive text is written with a Conflict Sequence arrowhead located about centrally in the Conflict Sequence region in mind. People whose arrowheads are close to the borders (within six points) of other Conflict Sequence regions may find that some text from the neighboring regions' descriptions is more accurate or useful.

While the following text describes the G-B-R Conflict Sequence, it should also be considered in light of the MVS of the person who has this Conflict Sequence. Since there are seven Motivational Value Systems, there are at least seven different ways to enter conflict and many different issues that can trigger conflict. These differences will affect the way people experience conflict and how they will resolve conflict. The first stage of this Conflict Sequence is Green. People with a short arrow whose MVS is also Green will experience a less noticeable transition from their MVS to the first stage of conflict than people whose MVS is a different color will.

## STAGE 1 GREEN CONFLICT

People in first stage Green conflict are motivated by a desire to carefully examine the situation. They want to be prudently cautious, checking and/or conserving resources and collecting information to make logical decisions.

They tend to minimize their feelings, instead focusing on non-emotional issues to clarify the conflict. If they do talk about feelings, they tend to say they feel uncertain or hesitant, or they say they are in need of more information. If coming from an MVS other than Green, they may feel a lower level of energy.

In first stage Green, people tend to take time and space to analyze the problem objectively. This may be perceived as pulling away from others or the issue; however, people in first stage Green are quietly and analytically engaged in the issue. They may prefer to be alone for a period of time to reflect on the issue and design a fair solution.

Productive first stage Green conflict behaviors are typically used in an effort to create rational, well thought-out solutions that are fair and unbiased. Greens' analysis is targeted at discovering facts or connections that were previously overlooked. The intent is to create better understanding and processes.

When unproductive, people in first stage Green may take too long to complete their analysis or overly focus on details. This may cause them to appear withdrawn or unconcerned about the problem. They may become rigidly adherent to certain principles and take a purely objective almost clinical approach to things.

### How People in Stage 1 Green Can Borrow Behavior to Be More Effective

People who are experiencing the first stage of conflict may act as described previously. However, people may also borrow behavior or examine their perceptions during conflict in an effort to be more effective.

In Stage 1 Green, people may be more effective if they:

- Ask people for their deadlines or reasons for urgency and negotiate a time for a decision.
- Analyze the emotions of others as additional data regarding the problem.

- Suggest a tentative, non-binding solution or involve other people in generating alternative scenarios.
- Consider delegating the issue or partnering with someone else.

## STAGE 2 BLUE CONFLICT

When an initial stand on logic, principles, and fairness is not effective at resolving the conflict, people who then move into the second stage of Blue (following Green) carry their analysis, data, information, and thought processes with them.

In the second stage of Blue (following Green), the needs of others are viewed as less important, and the primary motivation is to escape from the opposition without giving up anything of significant value. The desire for objectivity, fairness, and logic is replaced by a desire to give in for the moment and to let go of less important things. There is a feeling of justification in letting go of the preferred solution and allowing other people to have their way, because it is hoped that a small sacrifice will appease the other person and resolve the issue.

In the second stage of Blue (following Green), people tend to conditionally surrender, letting go of things that were deemed less important during their prior analysis.

Prepared with an abundance of logic and strategies, people in second stage Blue may choose to let their argument go, even encouraging others to try solutions that may be ineffective. They may use phrases such as "Whatever!" "I don't care; do what you want," or "If that's what you think… fine," to distance themselves from the decision and place accountability for negative outcomes on the other person. "Letting go" at this stage may be done deliberately to prevent the experience of moving into Stage 3 Red and potentially doing more damage.

People with a G-B-R Conflict Sequence generally work very hard in Stage 2 Blue to prevent going to Stage 3 Red. They may make larger and larger concessions in an effort to make the conflict go away, believing that the concessions are worth avoiding the discomfort and explosive potential of Stage 3 Red.

## STAGE 3 RED CONFLICT

In the third stage of Red (following Green and Blue), people tend to feel intensely angry, energized, and potentially out of control, demanding an "all or nothing" solution. They tend to feel that all of their efforts to resolve the issue logically and without confrontation have failed. They feel that the desired outcome must be forcibly taken from or forcibly denied to the other person, regardless of cost.

In the third stage of Red (following Green and Blue), people will typically challenge others or fight, potentially in an explosive manner. They may say that they no longer care what other people think or want, forcibly implementing whatever they originally thought was the best solution. If the conflict is severe, the relationship may be irreparably damaged by the harshness of personal attacks or by the negative reactions of people who view this third stage Red behavior as overblown and uncalled for.

### The Red Stage 3 Filter

Red is the third stage of conflict in the G-B-R sequence. While in first stage Green and observing Red behavior in another person, some projection of the third stage experience on others is possible. Assertive behavior in others may be perceived as irrational overreaction without first taking the time to consider the facts of the situation or the needs of others.

## CONFLICT RESOLUTION

Conflict is resolved when the elements of opposition are addressed and the people involved are able to return to feeling good about themselves again.

### The Path Back to the MVS from Stage 1 Green

Each person has a path back from conflict to their MVS and feelings of self-worth. Even though many people may feel and act similarly in the first stage of conflict, there may be differences that are related to the MVS they are trying to return to. Conflict management efforts can be improved by keeping these differences in mind.

The path back to the MVS will be different for every person. Table 3.8 features some general illustrations of the path from Stage 1 Green back to MVS.

**Figure 3.9** *Paths back to MVS from G-B-R*

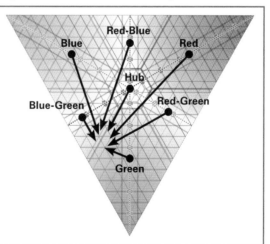

**Table 3.8** *Illustrations of the path back to MVS from Stage 1 Green*

| | |
|---|---|
| Blue MVS | Logically and fairly restoring harmony in the relationship |
| Red MVS | Collecting facts that can be used to accomplish tasks and goals |
| Green MVS | Clarifying principles and procedures that will restore order and assure a systematic solution |
| Red-Blue MVS | Creating a systematic way to assertively bring help to others |
| Red-Green MVS | Strengthening the strategy with additional facts and resources |
| Blue-Green MVS | Creating processes that help others help themselves |
| Hub MVS | Analytically generating options and making decisions that maintain future flexibility |

For more detailed information and ideas about resolving conflict with people who have this Conflict Sequence, also consult the "Productive Results of Conflict" sections in the chapters that describe the MVS of those people. No matter the MVS of people in the conflict, there are some things that can help them transition out of stage 1 Green.

## How to Approach People While They Are in Stage 1 Green Conflict

● Respect the person's need for time to think things through.

● Listen attentively, then repeat or paraphrase key points to prove you are listening.

● After listening, explain your point-of-view.

● Keep calm and unemotional, developing ideas in logical order.

- Listen to understand, not to respond.

- Focus on getting things right.

## THINGS TO AVOID WHEN APPROACHING PEOPLE WHILE THEY ARE IN STAGE 1 GREEN CONFLICT

- Focusing on the urgency of the issue or on how others feel about the problem.

- Challenging aggressively or using feelings to justify decisions.

- Forcing them to decide quickly or making the decision without their input.

# G-R-B

## CONFLICT SEQUENCE

This Conflict Sequence describes people who want to bring order and logic to the situation. If that does not work, they want to forcefully press for a logical resolution. If that does not work and others have more power in the situation, they may surrender.

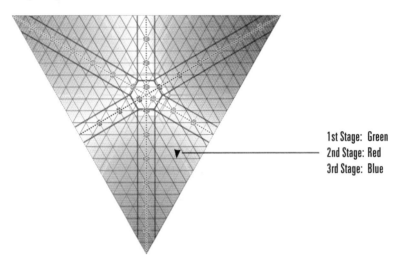

1st Stage: Green
2nd Stage: Red
3rd Stage: Blue

This descriptive text is written with a Conflict Sequence arrowhead located about centrally in the Conflict Sequence region in mind. People whose arrowheads are close to the borders (within six points) of other Conflict Sequence regions may find that some text from the neighboring regions' descriptions is more accurate or useful.

While the following text describes the G-R-B Conflict Sequence, it should also be considered in light of the MVS of the person who has this Conflict Sequence. Since there are seven Motivational Value Systems, there are at least seven different ways to enter conflict and many different issues that can trigger conflict. These differences will affect the way people experience conflict and how they will resolve conflict. The first stage of this Conflict Sequence is Green. People with a short arrow whose MVS is also Green will experience a less noticeable transition from their MVS to the first stage of conflict than people whose MVS is a different color will.

## STAGE 1 GREEN CONFLICT

People in first stage Green conflict are motivated by a desire to carefully examine the situation. They want to be prudently cautious, checking and/or conserving resources and collecting information to make logical decisions.

They tend to minimize their feelings, instead focusing on non-emotional issues to clarify the conflict. If they do talk about feelings, they tend to say they feel uncertain or hesitant, or they say they are in need of more information. If coming from an MVS other than Green, they may feel a lower level of energy.

In first stage Green, people tend to take time and space to analyze the problem objectively. This may be perceived as pulling away from others or the issue; however, people in first stage Green are quietly and analytically engaged in the issue. They may prefer to be alone for a period of time to reflect on the issue and design a fair solution.

Productive first stage Green conflict behaviors are typically used in an effort to create rational, well thought-out solutions that are fair and unbiased. Greens' analysis is targeted at discovering facts or connections that were previously overlooked. The intent is to create better understanding and processes.

When unproductive, people in first stage Green may take too long to complete their analysis or overly focus on details. This may cause them to appear withdrawn or unconcerned about the problem. They may become rigidly adherent to certain principles and take a purely objective almost clinical approach to things.

### How People in Stage 1 Green Can Borrow Behavior to Be More Effective

People who are experiencing the first stage of conflict may act as described previously. However, people may also borrow behavior or examine their perceptions during conflict in an effort to be more effective.

In Stage 1 Green, people may be more effective if they:

- Ask people for their deadlines or reasons for urgency and negotiate a time for a decision.

- Analyze the emotions of others as additional data regarding the problem.
- Suggest a tentative, non-binding solution or involve other people in generating alternative scenarios.
- Consider delegating the issue or partnering with someone else.

## STAGE 2 RED CONFLICT

When an initial stand on logic, principles, and fairness is not effective at resolving the conflict, people who then move into the second stage of Red (following Green) carry their analysis, data, information, and thought processes with them.

In the second stage of Red (following Green), the needs of others are viewed as less important, and the primary motivation is to forcefully implement the logical solution that was previously not accepted. The desire for objectivity, fairness, and logic is replaced by a strong desire to win. There is an increased confidence in their solution and a diminished regard for the impact of that solution on others. If the other party has to be defeated to achieve the win, it is seen as an acceptable outcome.

In the second stage of Red (following Green), people tend to become more energized and animated, forcefully arguing their position and using whatever powers or resources are available to implement their desired solution. Armed with an abundance of logic and strategies, people in second stage Red may issue ultimatums and attack issues and others in an effort to prove that they are right and force compliance. They may use strong and intentionally hurtful language in an attempt to force the other party to surrender, ensuring that they themselves do not have to surrender and move into their third stage of Blue.

People with a G-R-B Conflict Sequence generally work very hard in Stage 2 Red to prevent going to Stage 3 Blue. They may continue to elevate the importance and urgency of the situation and the intensity of their reaction. They may become increasingly forceful and directive, based on their earlier analysis, believing that the fight, regardless of the potential damage, is better than being forced to surrender in Stage 3 Blue.

## STAGE 3 BLUE CONFLICT

In the third stage of Blue (following Green and Red), people tend to feel completely defeated—not by others, but by the inability to find and implement a solution. They tend to feel that all of their efforts to resolve the issue logically and forcefully have failed. All that remains is to give up on the issue and figure out how to live with the pain of defeat.

In the third stage of Blue (following Green and Red), people will typically end their association with the issue and people. They may say that they no longer care about the conflict or the impact on the other people involved. If the conflict is severe, the relationship may be irreparably damaged, and they may refuse to become emotionally involved again with those other people.

### The Blue Stage 3 Filter

Blue is the third stage of conflict in the G-R-B sequence. When in first stage Green and observing Blue behavior in another person, some projection of the third stage experience onto others is possible. Accommodating behavior in others may be perceived as irrationally surrendering without first taking the time to collect the facts or to stand up for themselves.

## CONFLICT RESOLUTION

Conflict is resolved when the elements of opposition are addressed and the people involved are able to return to feeling good about themselves again.

### The Path Back to the MVS from Stage 1 Green

Each person has a path back from conflict to their MVS and feelings of self-worth. Even though many people may feel and act similarly in the first stage of conflict, there may be differences that are related to the MVS they are trying to return to. Conflict management efforts can be improved by keeping these differences in mind.

The path back to the MVS will be different for every person. Table 3.9 features some general illustrations of the path from Stage 1 Green back to MVS.

**Figure 3.10** *Paths back to MVS from G-R-B*

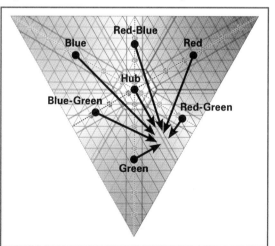

**Table 3.9** *Illustrations of the path back to MVS from Stage 1 Green*

| | |
|---|---|
| Blue MVS | Logically and fairly restoring harmony in the relationship |
| Red MVS | Collecting facts that can be used to accomplish tasks and goals |
| Green MVS | Clarifying principles and procedures that will restore order and assure a systematic solution |
| Red-Blue MVS | Creating a systematic way to assertively bring help to others |
| Red-Green MVS | Strengthening the strategy with additional facts and resources |
| Blue-Green MVS | Creating processes that help others help themselves |
| Hub MVS | Analytically generating options and making decisions that maintain future flexibility |

For more detailed information and ideas about resolving conflict with people who have this Conflict Sequence, also consult the "Productive Results of Conflict" sections in the chapters that describe the MVS of those people. No matter the MVS of people in the conflict, there are some things that can help them transition out of Stage 1 Green.

## HOW TO APPROACH PEOPLE WHILE THEY ARE IN STAGE 1 GREEN CONFLICT

● Respect the person's need for time to think things through.

● Listen attentively, repeat or paraphrase key points to prove you are listening.

● After listening, explain your point-of-view.

● Keep calm, unemotional, state ideas in a logical order.

- Listen to understand, not to respond.

- Focus on getting things right.

## THINGS TO AVOID WHEN APPROACHING PEOPLE WHILE THEY ARE IN STAGE 1 GREEN CONFLICT

- Focusing on the urgency of the issue or on how others feel about the problem.

- Challenging aggressively or using feelings to justify decisions.

- Forcing them to decide quickly or making the decision without their input.

# G-[BR]

## CONFLICT SEQUENCE

This Conflict Sequence describes people who want to maintain order and principles. If that does not work, they want to make a choice, depending on what's more reasonable in the situation: to give in with conditions or to forcefully engage.

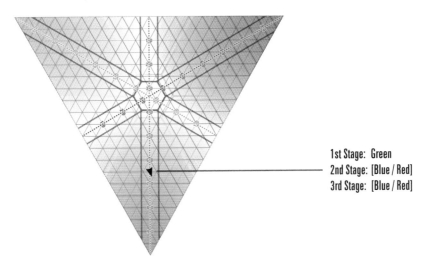

1st Stage: Green
2nd Stage: [Blue / Red]
3rd Stage: [Blue / Red]

This descriptive text is written with a Conflict Sequence arrowhead located centrally in the Conflict Sequence region in mind. People whose arrowheads are close to the borders (within six points) of other Conflict Sequence regions may find that some text from the neighboring regions' descriptions is more accurate or useful.

While the following text describes the G-[BR] Conflict Sequence, it should also be considered in light of the MVS of the person who has this Conflict Sequence. Since there are seven Motivational Value Systems, there are at least seven different ways to enter conflict and many different issues that can trigger conflict. These differences will affect the way people experience conflict and how they will resolve conflict. The first stage of this Conflict Sequence is Green. People with a short arrow whose MVS is also Green will experience a less noticeable transition from their MVS to the first stage of conflict than people whose MVS is a different color will.

## STAGE 1 GREEN CONFLICT

People in first stage Green conflict are motivated by a desire to carefully examine the situation. They want to be prudently cautious, checking and/or conserving resources and collecting information to make logical decisions.

They tend to minimize their feelings, instead focusing on non-emotional issues to clarify the conflict. If they do talk about feelings, they tend to say they feel uncertain or hesitant, or they say they are in need of more information. If coming from an MVS other than Green, they may feel a lower level of energy.

In first stage Green, people tend to take time and space to analyze the problem objectively. This may be perceived as pulling away from others or the issue; however, people in first stage Green are quietly and analytically engaged in the issue. They may prefer to be alone for a period of time to reflect on the issue and design a fair solution.

Productive first stage Green conflict behaviors are typically used in an effort to create rational, well thought-out solutions that are fair and unbiased. Greens' analysis is targeted at discovering facts or connections that were previously overlooked. The intent is to create better understanding and processes.

When unproductive, people in first stage Green may take too long to complete their analysis or overly focus on details. This may cause them to appear withdrawn or unconcerned about the problem. They may become rigidly adherent to certain principles and take a purely objective almost clinical approach to things.

### How People in Stage 1 Green Can Borrow Behavior to Be More Effective

People who are experiencing the first stage of conflict may act as described previously. However, people may also borrow behavior or examine their perceptions during conflict in an effort to be more effective.

In Stage 1 Green, people may be more effective if they:

- Ask people for their deadlines or reasons for urgency and negotiate a time for a decision.

- Analyze the emotions of others as additional data regarding the problem.

- Suggest a tentative, non-binding solution or involve other people in generating alternative scenarios.

- Consider delegating the issue or partnering with someone else.

## STAGE 2 BLEND OF BLUE & RED CONFLICT

When an initial stand on logic, principles and fairness is not effective at resolving the conflict, people who then move into the second stage of Blue/Red (following Green) carry their analysis, data, information, and thought processes with them.

People in this blended second and third stage may take different approaches, based on their perception of the situation. They may go to Blue followed by Red if the relationship is more important than the result or to Red followed by Blue if the result is more important than the relationship. In these cases, conflict can be understood more fully by referring to the G-B-R and G-R-B pages. It is also possible that the Red and Blue conflict stages will be combined for a blended conflict experience.

In the blended second and third stage of Blue/Red (following Green), the needs of others are viewed as less important, and the motivation is to persuade people to accept the most important parts of the logical solution that has already been identified. The desire for objectivity, fairness, and logic is replaced by a desire to strongly communicate and delegate tasks, seeking immediate action, so people can move on to other, more rational issues. There is a feeling of rightness in disregarding the input of others, because the solution will provide the final proof.

If they are unsuccessful in persuading others to act, they may forcefully restate their logic in an effort to overwhelm resistance, using phrases such as, "This is obviously the smartest thing to do," and, "Here's what you need to do."

## STAGE 3 BLEND OF BLUE & RED CONFLICT

While Blue and Red are blended in Stages 2 and 3, people will experience an internal difference between these stages. Stage 2 is characterized by a focus on the self and the problem, and Stage 3 is focused on the self. Therefore, the Stage 3 experience of Blue/Red is a more intense and self-focused version of the Stage 2 experience. If people concentrated on a conditionally accommodating, Blue approach in stage 2, their third stage is likely to be the explosive fighting typical of Stage 3 Red. If they concentrated on the assertive and argumentative

Red approach to Stage 2, their third stage is likely to be the painful defeat or surrender typical of Stage 3 Blue.

### The Blend of Blue & Red Stage 3 Filter

Red/Blue is the blended second and third stage of conflict in the G-[BR] sequence. While in first stage Green and observing Blue/Red behavior in another person, some projection of the second or third stage experience on the other is possible. Accommodating or confrontational behavior in others may be perceived as rash or irrational and not grounded in reality.

## CONFLICT RESOLUTION

Conflict is resolved when the elements of opposition are addressed and the people involved are able to return to feeling good about themselves again.

### The Path Back to the MVS from Stage 1 Green

Each person has a path back from conflict to their MVS and feelings of self-worth. Even though many people may feel and act similarly in the first stage of conflict, there may be differences that are related to the MVS they are trying to return to. Conflict management efforts can be improved by keeping these differences in mind.

**Figure 3.11** *Paths back to MVS from G-[RB]*

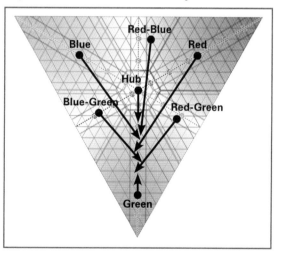

The path back to the MVS will be different for every person. Table 3.10 features some general illustrations of the path from Stage 1 Green back to MVS.

**Table 3.10** *Illustrations of the path back to MVS from Stage 1 Green*

| | |
|---|---|
| Blue MVS | Logically and fairly restoring harmony in the relationship |
| Red MVS | Collecting facts that can be used to accomplish tasks and goals |
| Green MVS | Clarifying principles and procedures that will restore order and assure a systematic solution |
| Red-Blue MVS | Creating a systematic way to assertively bring help to others |
| Red-Green MVS | Strengthening the strategy with additional facts and resources |
| Blue-Green MVS | Creating processes that help others help themselves |
| Hub MVS | Analytically generating options and making decisions that maintain future flexibility |

For more detailed information and ideas about resolving conflict with people who have this Conflict Sequence, also consult the "Productive Results of Conflict" sections in the chapters that describe the MVS of those people. No matter the MVS of people in the conflict, there are some things that can help them transition out of Stage 1 Green.

## HOW TO APPROACH PEOPLE WHILE THEY ARE IN STAGE 1 GREEN CONFLICT

- Respect the person's need for time to think things through.

- Listen attentively, then repeat or paraphrase key points to prove you are listening.

- After listening, explain your point-of-view.

- Keep calm and unemotional, developing ideas in logical order.

- Listen to understand, not to respond.

- Focus on getting things right.

## THINGS TO AVOID WHEN APPROACHING PEOPLE WHILE THEY ARE IN STAGE 1 GREEN CONFLICT

- Focusing on the urgency of the issue or on how others feel about the problem.

- Challenging aggressively or using feelings to justify decisions.

- Forcing them to decide quickly or making the decision without their input.

# [BR]-G
## CONFLICT SEQUENCE

This Conflict Sequence describes people who want to press assertively to maintain harmony and goodwill but do not want to sacrifice results for harmony. If that does not work, they may decide to withdraw from the situation.

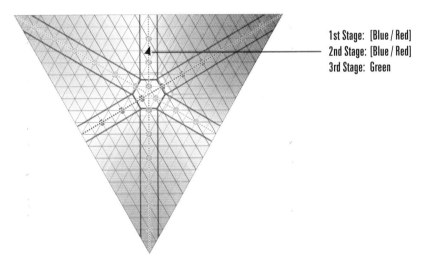

1st Stage: [Blue / Red]
2nd Stage: [Blue / Red]
3rd Stage: Green

This descriptive text is written with a Conflict Sequence arrowhead located centrally in the Conflict Sequence region in mind. People whose arrowheads are close to the borders (within six points) of other Conflict Sequence regions may find that some text from the neighboring regions' descriptions is more accurate or useful.

While the following text describes the [BR]-G Conflict Sequence, it should also be considered in light of the MVS of the person who has this Conflict Sequence. Since there are seven Motivational Value Systems, there are at least seven different ways to enter conflict and many different issues that can trigger conflict. These differences will affect the way people experience conflict and how they will resolve conflict. The first stage of this Conflict Sequence is a blend of Blue and Red. People with a short arrow whose MVS is also Red-Blue, will experience a less noticeable transition from their MVS to the first stage of conflict than people whose MVS is a different color will.

## STAGE 1 BLEND OF BLUE & RED CONFLICT

People in this blended first and second stage may take different approaches, based on their perception of the situation. They may go to Red followed by Blue if the results are at least temporarily more important than the relationships involved, or to Blue followed by Red if the relationships are more important than the results. In these cases, conflict can be understood more fully by referring to the B-R-G and R-G-B pages. It is also possible that the Red and Blue conflict stages will be combined for a blended conflict experience.

When Red and Blue are blended in the first stage of conflict, people are motivated to quickly and kindly find an acceptable solution. They want others to get along and end the conflict. They want to get a good result as soon as possible but do not want any solution to be implemented in an authoritarian, or domineering manner that would be hurtful to others.

They tend to feel alarmed when they are in conflict. To them, restoring the harmony in the relationship or team is a matter of greatest urgency. In addition to the conflict about the issue, people in the Red/Blue blend experience an internal tension between the two motivations of asserting and accommodating. The internal dilemma is about how to integrate their competing priorities in the conflict: performance versus people, results versus relationships.

They may attempt to mediate a conversation, so everyone's concerns can be aired. They sense what other people need and will accommodate their needs if possible or take up their cause and seek accommodation of their needs from others. They may act quickly, believing that others will benefit by following their advice.

When unproductive, they may attempt to force people to talk to each other or make decisions on others' behalf. This may cause them to appear intrusive or controlling. They may believe it is better to ask for forgiveness than for permission and they may appear unconcerned about the rules.

### How People in Stage 1 Blend of Blue & Red Can Borrow Behavior to Be More Effective

People who are experiencing the first stage of conflict may act as described previously. However, people may also borrow behavior or examine their perceptions during conflict in an effort to be more effective.

In a stage 1 and 2 blend of Blue/Red, people may be more effective if they:

- Take time to analyze as much detail about the issue as possible.
- Calmly state their personal priorities and boundaries.
- Consider whether others will view their actions as creating a precedent or a future obligation.
- Consider a Blue response when they feel Red, and a Red response when they feel Blue.

## STAGE 2 BLEND OF BLUE & RED CONFLICT

While Blue and Red are blended in Stages 1 and 2, people still experience a difference between Stage 1 and Stage 2. At first, they concentrate on themselves, the problem, and the other person. As the issue progresses to the second stage, they may drop the other person from focus, minimizing the importance of the other person's concerns and concentrating their energy on the problem and how it affects them. The second stage of conflict may appear similar to the first but it is a more intensely experienced and self-focused version of problem-solving than the first stage.

People with a [BR]-G Conflict Sequence generally work very hard to prevent going to Stage 3 Green. They may continue to elevate the importance and urgency of the situation and the degree of sacrifice they are willing to make to resolve it. They may believe that they are acting on their last chance to stay involved with a person or situation and that the struggle, no matter how difficult, is better than walking away in Stage 3 Green.

## STAGE 3 GREEN CONFLICT

In the third stage of Green (following a blend of Blue and Red) people tend to abandon or insulate themselves from feelings about the issue and the people involved. They tend to believe that their assertive and accommodating approaches to conflict have been met with a lack of cooperation or fair play and that no option remains, except to disengage.

In the third stage of Green (following a blend of Blue and Red) people will typically withdraw and cut off contact in order to preserve whatever they can from the situation. They may refuse to even talk about the past issue, because they think there is no remaining possibility of resolving it. If the conflict is severe, they may end the relationship and avoid all further interaction with the people involved.

### The Green Stage 3 Filter

Green is the third stage of conflict in the [BR]-G sequence. When in first stage Blue/Red and observing Green behavior in another person, some projection of the third stage experience on the other is possible. Analytical behavior in others may be perceived as abandonment or detachment without first taking a stand, sensing the needs of others, or engaging in problem solving efforts.

## CONFLICT RESOLUTION

Conflict is resolved when the elements of opposition are addressed and the people involved are able to return to feeling good about themselves again.

### The Path Back to the MVS from Stage 1 Blue/Red

Each person has a path back from conflict to their MVS and feelings of self-worth. Even though many people may feel and act similarly in the first stage of conflict, there may be differences that are related to the MVS they are trying to return to. Conflict management efforts can be improved by keeping these differences in mind.

The path back to the MVS will be different for every person. Table 3.11 features some general illustrations of the path from Stage 1 Blue/Red back to MVS.

**Figure 3.12** *Paths back to MVS from [BR]-G*

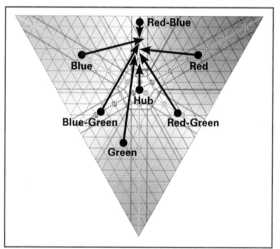

**Table 3.11** *Illustrations of the path back to MVS from Stage 1 Blue/Red*

| | |
|---|---|
| Blue MVS | Assertively restoring the peace and emphasizing the value of the relationship |
| Red MVS | Maintaining harmony and encouraging people to get behind a goal |
| Green MVS | Bringing people together to clarify objectives or processes |
| Red-Blue MVS | Pressing for harmony and refocusing on the need to develop others |
| Red-Green MVS | Collecting support and aligning people on strategy or tactics |
| Blue-Green MVS | Insisting on self-sufficiency for self and others |
| Hub MVS | Arguing kindly and persuasively to build consensus |

For more detailed information and ideas about resolving conflict with people who have this Conflict Sequence, also consult the "Productive Results of Conflict" sections in the chapters that describe the MVS of those people. No matter the MVS of people in the conflict, there are some things that can help them transition out of stage 1 Blue/Red.

## HOW TO APPROACH PEOPLE WHILE THEY ARE IN STAGE 1 BLEND OF BLUE & RED CONFLICT

● Acknowledge the need for action that maintains the relationship.

● Show willingness to consider or work with possible solutions.

● Be energetic and genuinely concerned.

● Focus conversation on the big picture and move forward for quick resolution.

- Respect or mirror the behavior you are witnessing. For example, if the person is dealing with the conflict situation in a Blue way, use the recommendations for Blue.

## THINGS TO AVOID WHEN APPROACHING PEOPLE WHILE THEY ARE IN STAGE 1 BLEND OF BLUE & RED CONFLICT

- Dismissing the issue as trivial or unimportant.

- Putting off resolving the conflict.

- Presenting a long, detailed analysis of the issue.

# [RG]-B
## CONFLICT SEQUENCE

This Conflict Sequence describes people who want to engage conflict quickly but indirectly, with thoughtful strategies. If that does not work and others have more power in the situation, they may surrender.

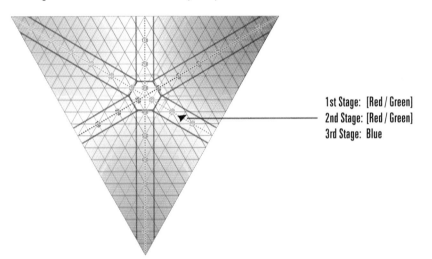

1st Stage: [Red / Green]
2nd Stage: [Red / Green]
3rd Stage: Blue

This descriptive text is written with a Conflict Sequence arrowhead located centrally in the Conflict Sequence region in mind. People whose arrowheads are close to the borders (within six points) of other Conflict Sequence regions may find that some text from the neighboring regions' descriptions is more accurate or useful.

While the following text describes the [RG]-B Conflict Sequence, it should also be considered in light of the MVS of the person who has this Conflict Sequence. Since there are seven Motivational Value Systems, there are at least seven different ways to enter conflict, and many different issues that can trigger conflict. These differences will affect the way people experience conflict and how they will resolve conflict. The first stage of this Conflict Sequence is a blend of

Red and Green. People with a short arrow whose MVS is also Red-Green will experience a less noticeable transition from their MVS to the first stage of conflict than people whose MVS is a different color will.

## STAGE 1 BLEND OF RED & GREEN CONFLICT

People in this blended first and second stage may take different approaches, based on their perception of the situation. They may go to Red followed by Green if the results are at least temporarily more important than the principles involved or to Green followed by Red if the principles are more important than the results. In these cases, conflict can be understood more fully by referring to the R-G-B and G-R-B pages. It is also possible that the Red and Green conflict stages will be combined for a blended conflict experience.

When Red and Green are blended in the first stage of conflict, people are motivated to quickly or fairly find a winning solution. They want to use their heads to win. They want to find a fair and rational solution to the problem, but they do not want rules enforced in ways that obstruct justifiable actions or results.

They tend to feel indignant when they are in conflict. To them, the facts of the matter are obvious and the right course of action is clear and urgent; they are frustrated when other people don't "get it." In addition to the conflict about the issue, people in the Red/Green blend experience an internal tension between the two motivations of asserting and analyzing. The internal dilemma is about how to integrate competing priorities in the conflict: performance vs. principles, results vs. rationality.

They prefer to take adequate time to think about the situation but also to act as quickly as reasonably possible. They engage others with well-crafted arguments that are intended to solidify their position and poke holes in the underlying assumptions of others' positions. They can be direct, believing that once the game is defined and the rules are clear, everyone can make their own decisions about how to compete.

When unproductive, they may engage in self-serving interpretations of rules or policy. This may cause them to appear manipulative or callous. They may become indignant or self-righteous and appear unconcerned about their effect on others.

**How People in Stage 1 Blend of Red & Green Can Borrow Behavior to Be More Effective**

People who are experiencing the first stage of conflict may act as described previously. However, people may also borrow behavior or examine their perceptions during conflict in an effort to be more effective.

In a Stage 1 and 2 blend of Red/Green, people may be more effective if they:

- Take time to consider the emotional impact their desired actions could have on other people.

- Inquire about the personal priorities and boundaries of others.

- Calculate the personal cost of a firm and unyielding stance toward others.

- Consider a Green response when they feel Red, and a Red response when they feel Green.

## STAGE 2 BLEND OF RED & GREEN CONFLICT

While Red and Green are blended in Stages 1 and 2, people still experience a difference between Stage 1 and Stage 2. At first, they concentrate on themselves, the problem, and the other person. As the issue progresses to the second stage, they may drop the other person from focus, minimizing the importance of the other person's concerns and concentrating their energy on the problem and how it affects them. The second stage of conflict may appear similar to the first, but it is a more intensely experienced and self-focused version of problem-solving than the first stage.

People with a [RG]-B Conflict Sequence generally work very hard to prevent going to Stage 3 Blue. They may continue to argue and investigate the situation to find information to support or challenge positions held by themselves and others. They may become rigid and antagonistic, believing that they are defending a case that, if lost, cannot be salvaged if they are forced to surrender in Stage 3 Blue.

## STAGE 3 BLUE CONFLICT

In the third stage of Blue (following a blend of Red and Green), people tend to feel completely defeated, not necessarily by others, but by the inability to find and implement a solution. They tend to feel that all of their efforts to resolve the issue logically and forcefully have failed, and all that remains is give up on the issue and figure out how to live with the pain of defeat.

In the third stage of Blue (following a blend of Red and Green), people will typically end association with the issue and others. They may say they no longer care about the conflict or the impact on the people involved. If the conflict is severe, the relationship may be irreparably damaged by the inability to *ever* become emotionally committed again.

### The Blue Stage 3 Filter

Blue is the third stage of conflict in the [RG]-B sequence. When in first stage Red/Green and observing Blue behavior in another person, some projection of the third stage experience onto the other is possible. Accommodating behavior of others may be perceived as spineless or lacking commitment or intelligence, without any attempt to defend or assert their rights.

## CONFLICT RESOLUTION

Conflict is resolved when the elements of opposition are addressed and the people involved are able to return to feeling good about themselves again.

### The Path Back to the MVS from Stage 1 Red/Green

Each person has a path back from conflict to their MVS and feelings of self-worth. Even though many people may feel and act similarly in the first stage of conflict, there may be differences that are related to the MVS they are trying to return to. Conflict management efforts can be improved by keeping these differences in mind.

**Figure 3.13** *Paths back to MVS from [RG]-B*

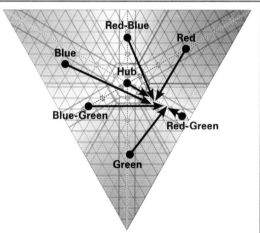

The path back to the MVS will be different for every person. Table 3.12 features some general illustrations of the path from Stage 1 Red/Green back to MVS.

**Table 3.12** *Illustrations of the path back to MVS from Stage 1 Red/Green*

| | |
|---|---|
| Blue MVS | Taking quick, logical action that brings help to others |
| Red MVS | Using the rules judiciously to produce results |
| Green MVS | Finding a flaw in a system and acting to improve that system |
| Red-Blue MVS | Clearly defining and dismantling the barriers to the growth of others |
| Red-Green MVS | Solidifying a position with additional evidence and action |
| Blue-Green MVS | Taking a strong and logical stand that enhances justice and equality |
| Hub MVS | Appropriately bending the rules to fit the situation |

For more detailed information and ideas about resolving conflict with people who have this Conflict Sequence, also consult the "Productive Results of Conflict" sections in the chapters that describe the MVS of those people. No matter the MVS of people in the conflict, there are some things that can help them transition out of Stage 1 Red/Green.

## HOW TO APPROACH PEOPLE WHILE THEY ARE IN STAGE 1 BLEND OF RED & GREEN CONFLICT

- Listen and restate to prove your understanding.

- Acknowledge the need for a quick and logical response.

- Allow time for reflection, but maintain focus on resolution.

- Keep conversation rational and unemotional.

- Respect or mirror the behavior you are witnessing. For example, if the person is dealing with the conflict situation in a Red way, use the recommendations for Red.

## THINGS TO AVOID WHEN APPROACHING PEOPLE WHILE THEY ARE IN STAGE 1 BLEND OF RED & GREEN CONFLICT

- Minimizing the issue or dismissing it as trivial or unimportant.

- Responding without confidence or in an overly emotional manner.

- Avoiding the issue or thinking that the problem will go away on its own.

# [BG]-R
## CONFLICT SEQUENCE

This Conflict Sequence describes people who want to maintain peace and harmony but with caution regarding the personal costs of doing so. If that does not work, they may feel compelled to fight, possibly in an explosive manner.

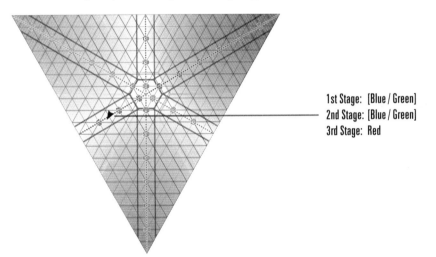

1st Stage: [Blue / Green]
2nd Stage: [Blue / Green]
3rd Stage: Red

This descriptive text is written with a Conflict Sequence arrowhead located centrally in the Conflict Sequence region in mind. People whose arrowheads are close to the borders (within six points) of other Conflict Sequence regions may find that some text from the neighboring regions' descriptions is more accurate or useful.

While the following text describes the [BG]-R Conflict Sequence, it should also be considered in light of the MVS of the person who has this Conflict Sequence. Since there are seven Motivational Value Systems, there are at least seven different ways to enter conflict and many different issues that can trigger conflict. These differences will affect the way people experience conflict and how they will resolve conflict. The first stage of this Conflict Sequence is a blend of

Blue and Green. People with a short arrow whose MVS is also Blue-Green will experience a less noticeable transition from their MVS to the first stage of conflict than people whose MVS is a different color will.

## STAGE 1 BLEND OF BLUE & GREEN CONFLICT

People in this blended first and second stage may take different approaches, based on their perception of the situation. They may go to Blue followed by Green if the relationships are more important than the principles involved or to Green followed by Blue if the principles are more important than the relationships. In these cases, conflict can be understood more fully by referring to the B-G-R and G-B-R pages. It is also possible that the Blue and Green conflict stages will be combined for a blended conflict experience.

When Blue and Green are blended in the first stage of conflict, people are motivated to maintain peace and harmony and to minimize the personal cost of doing so. They want to find a fair and rational solution to the problem, but they do not want rules enforced in ways that would be harmful or unjust to anyone involved in the conflict.

They tend to feel surprised that they are in conflict. The moment they realize it may sometimes be described as a "deer in the headlights" experience, accompanied by similar body language. In addition to the conflict about the issue, people in the Blue/Green blend experience an internal tension between the two motivations of accommodating and analyzing. The internal dilemma is about how to integrate their competing priorities in the conflict: people versus principles, reason versus relationships.

They prefer to take time to think about the situation, and their thoughts include the feelings and concerns of others. They ask questions about how the conflict started, whether it was warranted, what other people truly want, and what can be learned from the situation. They attempt to uncover the source of the misunderstanding, believing that if assumptions or intentions are clarified, understanding will result, and harmony will be restored.

When unproductive, they may become overly passive. This may cause them to appear unconcerned or incapable of addressing the problem. They may apologize excessively or isolate themselves from the problem, so they can wait it out.

**How People in Stage 1 Blend of Blue & Green Can Borrow Behavior to Be More Effective**

People who are experiencing the first stage of conflict may act as described previously. However, people may also borrow behavior or examine their perceptions during conflict in an effort to be more effective.

In a Stage 1 and 2 blend of Blue/Green, people may be more effective if they:

- Focus on what to do next, instead of analyzing the sequence of events that led to the conflict.

- Clearly state their personal priorities, boundaries, and limits.

- Ask other people to suggest a potential solution as a starting point.

- Consider a Green response when they feel Blue, and a Blue response when they feel Green.

## STAGE 2 BLEND OF BLUE & GREEN CONFLICT

While Blue and Green are blended in Stages 1 and 2, people still experience a difference between Stage 1 and Stage 2. At first, they concentrate on themselves, the problem, and the other person. As the issue progresses to the second stage, they may drop the other person from focus, minimizing the importance of the other person's concerns and concentrating their energy on the problem and how it affects them. The second stage of conflict may appear similar to the first, but it is a more intensely experienced and self-focused version of problem-solving than the first stage.

People with a [BG]-R Conflict Sequence generally work very hard to prevent going to Stage 3 Red. They may make larger and larger concessions or engage in complex rationalizations in an effort to make the conflict go away, believing that no situation or person should be capable of provoking them to respond in the explosive and potentially hurtful manner of their third stage Red.

## STAGE 3 RED CONFLICT

In the third stage of Red (following a blend of Blue and Green), people tend to feel intensely angry, energized, and potentially out of control, demanding an "all or nothing" solution. They tend to feel that all of their efforts to resolve the issue logically and without confrontation have failed. They feel that the desired outcome must be forcibly taken from or forcibly denied to the other person, regardless of cost.

In the third stage of Red (following a blend of Blue and Green) people will typically challenge others or fight, potentially in an explosive manner. They may say they no longer care what other people think or want, forcibly implementing whatever they originally thought was the best solution. If the conflict is severe, the relationship may be irreparably damaged by the harshness of personal attacks or by the negative reactions of people who view this third stage Red behavior as overblown and uncalled for.

### The Red Stage 3 Filter

Red is the third stage of conflict in the [BG]-R sequence. When in first stage Blue/Green and observing Red behavior in another person, some projection of the third stage experience on the other is possible. Assertive behavior in others may be perceived as angry over-reaction without first taking the time to consider the facts of the situation or the needs of others.

## CONFLICT RESOLUTION

Conflict is resolved when the elements of opposition are addressed and the people involved are able to return to feeling good about themselves again.

### The Path Back to the MVS from Stage 1 Blue/Green

Each person has a path back from conflict to their MVS and feelings of self-worth. Even though many people may feel and act similarly in the first stage of conflict, there may be differences that are related to the MVS they are trying to return to. Conflict management efforts can be improved by keeping these differences in mind.

The path back to the MVS will be different for every person. Table 3.13 features some general illustrations of the path from Stage 1 Blue/Green back to MVS.

**Figure 3.14** *Paths back to MVS from [BG]-R*

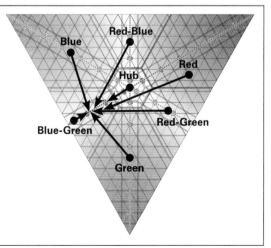

**Table 3.13** *Illustrations of the path back to MVS from Stage 1 Blue/Green*

| | |
|---|---|
| Blue MVS | Identifying the rights of others and seeing that they are supported |
| Red MVS | Clarifying issues and values and refocusing on action |
| Green MVS | Considering the logic of others and clarifying the process |
| Red-Blue MVS | Carefully considering the capabilities and potential of others |
| Red-Green MVS | Revising the strategy and improving the odds of its success |
| Blue-Green MVS | Reaffirming the value of people and principles |
| Hub MVS | Clarifying the rules of interaction and building consensus |

For more detailed information and ideas about resolving conflict with people who have this Conflict Sequence, also consult the "Productive Results of Conflict" sections in the chapters that describe the MVS of those people. No matter the MVS of people in the conflict, there are some things that can help them transition out of Stage 1 Blue/Green.

## How to Approach People While They Are in Stage 1 Blend of Blue & Green Conflict

- Look for a reasonable solution that also maintains harmony.

- Make genuine inquiry about their welfare and how the conflict is affecting them.

- Depersonalize the problem, reassuring them that the relationship is intact.

- Allow time for consideration, reframing mistakes or problems as learning opportunities.

- Respect or mirror the behavior you are witnessing. For example, if the person is dealing with the conflict situation in a Green way, use the recommendations for Green.

## THINGS TO AVOID WHEN APPROACHING PEOPLE WHILE THEY ARE IN STAGE 1 BLEND OF BLUE & GREEN CONFLICT

- Pushing for an answer without allowing time to think.

- Dictating solutions to conflict and using power to control the outcome.

- Raising your voice and appearing aggressive or overly competitive.

# [BRG]
## CONFLICT SEQUENCE

This Conflict Sequence describes people who want to determine the most appropriate response to each situation and to experiment with accommodating, assertive, and analytical approaches. If that does not work, they may feel compelled to use a non-preferred approach.

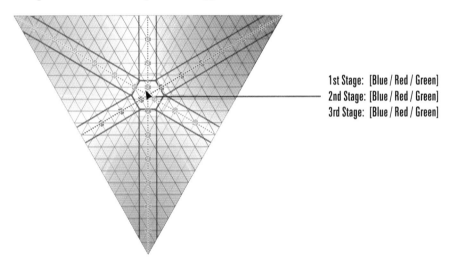

1st Stage:  [Blue / Red / Green]
2nd Stage:  [Blue / Red / Green]
3rd Stage:  [Blue / Red / Green]

This descriptive text is written with a Conflict Sequence arrowhead located centrally in the Conflict Sequence region in mind. People whose arrowheads are close to the borders (within six points) of other Conflict Sequence regions may find that some text from the neighboring regions' descriptions is more accurate or useful.

While the following text describes the [BRG] Conflict Sequence, it should also be considered in light of the MVS of the person who has this Conflict Sequence. Since there are seven Motivational Value Systems, there are at least seven different ways to enter conflict and many different issues that can trigger conflict. These differences will affect the way people experience conflict and how they will resolve conflict. The first stage of this Conflict Sequence is a blend of Blue, Red, and Green. People with a short arrow whose MVS is Hub will experience a less noticeable transition from their MVS to the first stage of conflict than people whose MVS is a different color will.

## STAGE 1 BLEND OF BLUE, RED, & GREEN CONFLICT

When all three stages and motives are blended in a [BRG] Conflict Sequence, people prefer to remain flexible in the way they approach each conflict situation. They want to come up with tailored solutions for those involved. They address each conflict differently, depending on the situation and circumstances.

In conflict, they may experience a range of emotions about conflict, depending on where it occurs and with whom it happens. Unlike others, whose motives are experienced in a predictable sequence during conflict, their motives in conflict all feel about equal. Instead of a predictable response, their behavior may reflect the way that others approach them. In each situation, they decide how to respond depending on the circumstances. They are natural problem solvers and tend to believe there isn't any challenge that doesn't have a solution. They are willing to keep trying different solutions until one works.

In conflict, they define the context in which to consider any problem. The context may include a combination of variables, such as the value of the relationship, the importance of the issue, or the environment in which the conflict occurs. Once the context is defined, the appropriate response can be selected.

When unproductive, they may show the sacrifice of Blue, the argumentativeness of Red, or the detachment of Green. They may also alternate between approaches and appear non-committal. This behavior may prove confusing to others and lead to the belief that the only thing truly predictable about them in conflict is that they are *not* predictable.

### How People in Stage 1 Blend of Blue, Red, & Green Can Borrow Behavior to Be More Effective

People who are experiencing the first stage of conflict may act as described previously. However, people may also borrow behavior or examine their perceptions during conflict in an effort to be more effective.

When all three colors blend in Stage 1, people may be more effective if they:

- Challenge their assumptions about why they are responding to conflict in a particular way.
- Clearly state their point-of-view as it relates to each specific situation.
- Let other people know where they are coming from with regards to each situation.

## STAGE 2 BLEND OF BLUE, RED, & GREEN CONFLICT

When all three colors are blended, people will generally address conflict in flexible, situationally dependent ways throughout all three stages. However, there is a difference between this approach in Stage 2 because it is characterized by a focus on the problem and the self and less emphasis is given to the needs of others. Stage 2 may take the form of conditional accommodation, fighting, or arguing against others, or it might be independent analysis of the situation.

## STAGE 3 BLEND OF BLUE, RED, & GREEN CONFLICT

While the situationally dependent response to conflict continues into Stage 3, there is a difference between this approach and Stage 2 because Stage 3 is characterized by a focus on the self and less emphasis is given to the needs of others and the problem at hand. Stage 3 may take the form of the least desired approach to the specific situation. It may look and feel like the unconditional surrender of Stage 3 Blue, the fighting for survival of Stage 3 Red, or the total withdrawal of Stage 3 Green.

### The Blend of Blue, Red, & Green Stage 3 Filter

People with a [BRG] Conflict Sequence can experience any color as their third stage of conflict. While they are in conflict, they may perceive that other people with a clear first stage are inflexible and not able to adapt to the situation. They may think that people in Stage 1 Blue are blinded by emotion, believe that others in Stage 1 Red are impulsive, and think that others in Stage 1 Green are uncommunicative.

## CONFLICT RESOLUTION

Conflict is resolved when the elements of opposition are addressed and the people involved are able to return to feeling good about themselves again.

**The Path Back to the MVS from Stage 1 Blend of Blue, Red, & Green**

Each person has a path back from conflict to their MVS and feelings of self-worth. Even though many people may feel and act similarly in the first stage of conflict, there may be differences that are related to the MVS they are trying to return to. Conflict management effort can be improved by keeping these differences in mind.

The path back to the MVS will be different for every person. Table 3.14 features some general illustrations of the path from Stage 1 blend of Blue, Red, & Green back to MVS.

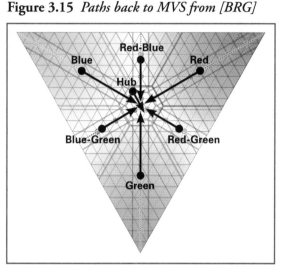

**Figure 3.15** *Paths back to MVS from [BRG]*

**Table 3.14** *Illustrations of the path back to MVS from Stage 1 [BRG]*

| | |
|---|---|
| Blue MVS | Going along with the option that is the least burdensome to others |
| Red MVS | Acting on the option most likely to succeed |
| Green MVS | Considering all the alternatives and selecting the most logical approach |
| Red-Blue MVS | Determining the best way forward for both parties |
| Red-Green MVS | Advancing the strategy in the best way possible for the situation |
| Blue-Green MVS | Searching for the best way to maintain self-sufficiency |
| Hub MVS | Experimenting with different approaches that do not restrict future options |

For more detailed information and ideas about resolving conflict with people who have this Conflict Sequence, also consult the "Productive Results of Conflict" sections in the chapters that describe the MVS of those people. No matter the MVS of people in the conflict, there are some things that can help them transition out of Stage 1 [BRG].

## How to Approach People While They Are in Stage 1 Blend of Blue, Red, & Green Conflict

- Ask them to clarify the process and where they are "coming from" on the issue.

- Be open to their point of view and their potential solutions.

- Be willing to explore the situation as a unique situation.

- Respect or mirror the behavior you are witnessing. For example, if the person is dealing with the conflict situation in a Blue way, use the recommendations for Blue.

- Ask open-ended questions that will encourage them to clarify how they see this issue at this time.

## Things to Avoid When Approaching People While They Are In Stage 1 Blend of Blue, Red, & Green Conflict

- Limiting ideas and showing lack of concern for the issue.

- Being rigid and dogmatic or not mirroring their approach.

- Expecting consistency in responses across multiple situations.

## GOING FURTHER

# SDI Applications

The SDI is about relationships—and relationships are everywhere. The SDI is most frequently used as the relationship improvement part of any training or development initiative. Whenever and wherever people need to work together effectively, the SDI can help. Following are some examples of typical SDI applications:

## APPRECIATIVE INQUIRY

When was the last time you were at your best at work? What brings you a sense of self-worth? These questions are part of appreciative inquiry and a perfect fit for the SDI. In an appreciative inquiry framework, the SDI provides a language to find out whether people feel they can bring their "best self" to work—or whether they believe they borrow behavior to be effective, or feel forced into a Mask Relating Style at work.

## BOARD DEVELOPMENT

Boards that use the SDI benefit from improved clarity in communication, less time spent in unproductive conflict, and better results from conflicts. The very idea of a board is to assemble committed experts with diverse backgrounds, perspectives, opinions, and ideas, then jointly determine the best course of action. Boards should encourage opposition, recognize it for what it is, and address it for the improvement of the organization. The SDI gives board members a language to differentiate conflict from opposition and a common language to help make decisions consistent with their values.

## Change Management

People may resist or embrace change for different reasons. Change Management training that integrates the SDI can help those responsible for the changes anticipate resistance and plan engagement strategies. People who are affected by the change can identify where their own resistance is coming from and manage this more productively. In SDI terms, Blues may resist change that negatively affects others, but embrace change that demonstrates a clear regard for people. Greens may resist change that is not well thought through or properly researched, but embrace change that is rational and realistic. The list goes on for each MVS. Many people manifest their resistance to change by entering conflict. It is at this critical juncture that change efforts are won or lost. If conflict can be anticipated and prevented, needed change can happen; if conflict is avoided or allowed to progress into the second or third stage it will most likely fail to meet its objectives.

## Coaching

Coaches need to understand the motives and values of their clients. One of the first tasks for a coach is to assess the client's Motivational Value System and Conflict Sequence and to help the client see their connections to and alignment with the situation about which they are being coached. From there, the focus shifts to improving the person's performance in relating to others, both when things are going well and during conflict. The *Portrait of Personal Strengths* becomes a metaphorical toolbox for coaches, and the coach can help clients fully consider their choices. Coaching can range from a formal relationship over years to an informal follow-up after a workshop, meant to reinforce learning and encourage the implementation of action plans created at the workshop.

## Communication

Organizations that use the SDI get the benefit of enhanced communication, whether they do formal communication training or not. The SDI gives people a language for relationships. It helps them talk about motives, values, intentions, threats to self-worth, and other topics that might otherwise be omitted from conversations. People remember the results of the SDI and quickly adopt the terms to describe what's happening between individuals and groups. Statements like, "That was a really Green presentation," or, "I need to borrow some Blue strengths for my next customer meeting," are sure signs that Relationship Awareness is taking hold. Communication training with the SDI often focuses on the preferred style of sending (encoding) and receiving (decoding) messages and the importance of understanding the internal filters that people use to evaluate messages.

## Conflict Management

Conflict is a fact of life for individuals, organizations, and societies. The costs of conflict are well documented and include high turnover, grievances and lawsuits, absenteeism, divorce, dysfunctional families, prejudice, and fear. Many people don't realize that well-managed conflict can be a force for positive change. Conflict is an opportunity to learn. People only experience conflict about things that are important to them, so every conflict includes an opportunity to learn about people's values and priorities. Relationship Awareness tools help people identify the source of their conflict, manage it more effectively, and reach a true resolution that also strengthens relationships.

## Counseling

The Strength Deployment Inventory has been used widely in a variety of counseling settings, including schools and in individual, group, marriage, and family therapy. The SDI is unique, because it provides insights into people's underlying motivations, both when things are going well and when people have encountered conflict or opposition. The positive psychology behind the SDI is ideal to help people assess their self-concepts, from which behavior flows. People who are concerned about some unproductive behaviors may be able to reorganize their self-concepts and include the idea that they are striving for self-worth. More productive behaviors flow from a more productive self-concept.

## Crew Resource Management

Crew Resource Management (CRM) training with the SDI helps crew members gain greater influence over the human factors that contribute to critical incidents. While this training originated with airlines and flight safety, its applicability to other industries, such as health care, cruise-ships and cargo shipping, and manufacturing, is gaining recognition, because it focuses on the human factors that contribute to costly errors in high reliability environments. Emergency response teams, police and fire departments, and forestry services all benefit from reducing the human factors in errors. When individual motives and Conflict Sequences are considered as a part of CRM training, all members of the crew get an idea of how they will respond individually and collectively. With this knowledge, crews can agree in advance about who will do what in the event of a critical incident. When the expectations are clear, members of the crew can create plans about how to borrow behavior and manage potential incidents more effectively.

## CUSTOMER SERVICE

Do all customers really expect the same thing, or might Blues prefer a different experience than Red-Greens prefer? Customer service personnel who are aware of these differences can more readily recognize them and adjust their service style to these customers. When things go wrong, service personnel are the face of the organization and the embodiment of the brand. How they treat a customer in difficult situations can make the difference between a negative review and a customer for life.

## DECISION MAKING

Do Reds, Hubs, and Blue-Greens make decisions in different ways? When important decisions are considered by MVS groups, each group will likely identify key factors that other groups could overlook. An integrative dialogue after sub-group processing can more clearly define the context for the decision and the factors to be considered, and it will ideally result in higher quality decisions that can be supported more widely.

## DIVERSITY TRAINING

Diversity training with the SDI involves the diversity of motivation. When using the SDI in traditional diversity training, groups are formed based on SDI results. Invariably, people with very different appearances, beliefs, and backgrounds will work together and find that underneath the traditional or physically obvious differences, they share some common motivations. Similarly, people who might otherwise appear very similar may find great diversity in their motives. Motivational types add a new dimension to diversity training, one that also has the power to form stronger relationships. When diversity issues are related to interpersonal conflict, the conflict management experiences based on SDI results can help to open up a respectful dialogue.

## EMOTIONAL INTELLIGENCE

Emotional Intelligence is a set of skills in four domains: 1) Self-Awareness, 2) Self-Management, 3) Interpersonal Awareness, and 4) Relationship Management. The SDI excels at generating awareness, which leads to greater acceptance and appreciation of others and ultimately to greater effectiveness. SDI has been integrated with behavioral competency frameworks to demonstrate how it can contribute to the development of emotional intelligence skills.

## EMPLOYEE ENGAGEMENT

Do you love what you do? People who find their work fulfilling typically say that their work uses their strengths, is meaningful, and connects with their sense of purpose. The SDI helps people create conditions in which they feel free to use their strengths and engage in dialogue about how people can find meaning in their work.

## FICTIONAL CHARACTER DEVELOPMENT

Have you heard an actor or actress ask "What's my motivation?" The SDI can be used to answer that question. It can be used to help define fictional characters that are realistic and consistent. Knowing the MVS and Conflict Sequence of a character makes it easy to think about what the character will want to do in any given situation. When authors, screenwriters, cartoonists, playwrights, and performers understand what the SDI suggests for their own relationships, they can apply those ideas to their characters. Some facilitators like to provide examples of Red, Green, Blue, and Hub characters from movies or popular television shows.

## IMPROVEMENT EFFORTS

Whether an organization is focused on continuous improvement, or project based improvements, people with different Motivational Value Systems will have different ideas about what should count as improvements. The SDI can help facilitate dialogue about the meaning of results and highlight the different filters at play. When there is tension between processes, outcomes, and the effects on people, there is the potential for interpersonal conflict. Improvement teams who are aware of each other's MVSs and Conflict Sequences will be prepared to anticipate and prevent much of the conflict that might otherwise occur.

## LEADERSHIP DEVELOPMENT

Leadership is a relationship. The SDI helps leaders increase their awareness of their leadership style, both when things are going well and during conflict. To create trust with a sometimes skeptical workforce, leaders need to communicate clearly and consistently about who they are, their philosophy of leadership, and their definition of results. They also need to understand the values and attitudes of the people they hope to lead, so they can create conditions in which others can develop and succeed.

## MEDIATION TRAINING

The SDI is used both in training mediators and during formal mediation with the disputing parties. Mediators learn to recognize conflict stages in other people, so they can focus discussion on returning the parties involved to a place where they feel good about themselves again. Mediators may call for a private caucus if they perceive that one of the parties is in Stage two conflict (and that the other party is out of focus) and work to individually return that person to the first stage of conflict so they can resolve the dispute with all parties' interests in mind. When the SDI is used with the parties to the dispute, it often leads to discussions that help the parties understand each other's perspectives and intentions more clearly. This understanding contributes to more rapid and acceptable results in the mediation. In some cases, disputing parties acknowledge that the whole thing was really an unwarranted conflict that got blown out of proportion. If they had recognized it earlier, there would have been no dispute at all.

## ORGANIZATIONAL CULTURE

Organizations and even departments or divisions within them have a certain feel or culture. It's "the way we do things around here" that distinguishes them from other organizations. The SDI fits into organizational culture training by helping employees connect their individual values to the organization's values. Some organizations look at groups of SDI results and spot trends or patterns that prompt them to take action. They may find that their recruitment practices are targeted at certain types of people to the point that personality type diversity within the organization is limited. Other findings include the identification of subgroups with markedly different results when things are going well or during conflict. When the SDI language of relationships becomes part of the culture, SDI training can be part of new employee orientation.

## PROJECT MANAGEMENT

Most projects are team-based. Most project failures have nothing to do with the plan; they are the result of poor relationships among the team members. Deadlines and deliverables are the focus of most team projects. But timelines, flowcharts, and software can't ensure that a project will be completed on time or that a high-quality result will be delivered. To have projects run smoothly and produce deliverables on time, project teams need to be able to collaborate effectively. Project team members need to understand what drives all team members and manage themselves through the conflicts that will inevitably occur during the project. Relationships within teams are one of the key ingredients in successful project management.

## SALES TRAINING

The SDI helps salespeople see that the key to a successful sales career lies in being able to relate to people on their own terms. Many salespeople believe that in order to sell, they need to use techniques that turn prospects into customers. Relationship Awareness shows that in order to appeal to potential customers, one needs to speak to them in their own language and show the benefits that they care about in a way that they understand. In short, the language of SDI helps salespeople tailor communication styles to each customer.

## SCHOOL TRANSITION

Whether students are moving from school to work, high school to college, junior college to university, or any of a number of other transitions, the SDI can help guide the transition and contribute to a better outcome. Students can examine their personal purpose and values and consider different fields of study or work where they can flourish. They can identify relationships that are critical to their success and those that might hinder their progress. With this understanding, they can create a plan to reach their educational and career aspirations.

## SCHOOL VIOLENCE PREVENTION AND ANTI-BULLYING TRAINING

Unresolved conflict and the devaluing of others is at the heart of bullying and violence in our schools. The SDI gives young people a way to understand that conflict is a threat to self-worth and a way to turn conflict into a positive force that can be used to solve problems. Young people who learn to see the value in others and in themselves are more likely to invest time and energy in resolving conflict for the benefit of all parties. It's hard to dislike a person whom you really know. The SDI helps students get to know themselves first—and then each other.

## STRATEGIC DIALOGUE

Strategy needs to be based on purpose and practical values. A discussion of organizational purpose leads to a discussion of and alignment with individuals' personal purposes and values. Different people will place different values on the results the organization produces, and these differences can contribute to better strategic dialogue. Many strategic planning sessions that integrate the SDI do so at the beginning of the meetings or as pre-work. The team triangle is on display during the planning, so team members can be reminded of everyone's motives, values, and Conflict Sequences.

## TEAM BUILDING

The SDI accelerates team development. It provides a common language for *Forming* teams and tools to help them through the *Storming* stage so they can more quickly move on to *Norming* and *Performing*. Team-building efforts with the SDI are often integrated with other efforts within the organization. Teams can be guided through a series of experiences intended to raise members' awareness of motives and Conflict Sequences for themselves and the other team members. Whether conducted in a classroom setting, during a retreat, or at an adventure-learning location, the SDI is the catalyst for learning that participants remember and apply.

## TIME MANAGEMENT

People with different motives and values may have different techniques and time traps. For example, there can be tension between the "do it now" preference of Reds and the "do it right" preference of Greens. Blues may succumb to the time-trap of helping others to the point of being unable to perform their own work, while Hubs may succumb to the time trap of holding all options open and failing to commit to a course of action. While no one can really manage time, they can manage events and activities in time. The SDI can shine a light on different strategies and help people learn from each other.

# The SDI View of Personality

This chapter explores some of the debates about personality theory and embeds answers to frequently asked questions about the SDI within those debates. It has a more academic tone than the balance of this book and makes references to several sources that, if the reader is so inspired, will facilitate a deeper consideration of these issues.

The questions explored in this section are:

1. What are personality types?

2. Is personality the result of nature or nurture?

3. Is the person or the situation responsible for behavior?

4. Does personality change?

## What Are Personality Types?

The SDI describes seven Motivational Value Systems and 13 Conflict Sequences. These are personality types.

The study of personality invites classification of persons into categories or types. As Kluckhohn and Murray (1948) noted, every person is like all other persons, like some other persons, and like no other person. Personality types result from an attempt to explain this middle ground of how persons are similar to some other persons. The fact that people can be described as having the same personality type in no way invalidates their uniqueness; people of the same type still have significant differences from each other. Personality is "a stable set of tendencies and characteristics that determine those commonalities and differences in people's psychological behavior (thoughts, feelings, and actions) that have continuity in time and that may not be easily understood as the sole result of social and biological pressures of the moment" (Maddi, 1996, p. 6).

"Any representation of personality is a hypothetical formulation, not a record of facts" (Murray & Kluckhohn, 1948, p. 6). How, then, is the concept of personality types to be described in ways that are meaningful and useful to individual people, yet still acceptable and useful for organizations and researchers? The underlying question here is: What should count as evidence of personality? There is philosophical tension between theorizing and measuring, between concepts and statistics, between subjective and objective data (Rosenberg, 2008). While no one is arguing one side to the exclusion of the other, there are differences in emphasis. Some academicians recommend that personality theory be taught as science, rather than as history courses. They recommend that students of personality theory should know the grand theories of personality, as well as whether these theories are supported by measurement-based evidence (McCrae, 2011). Two of the grand theorists are Sigmund Freud and Carl Jung.

### Freud's Typology

Sigmund Freud is best known for the development of psychoanalysis, and the character types he described, based on patients' successful development or fixation at a stage in development (Freud, 1923/1961). However, he was also interested in normal people. Near the end of his career, he modified his conception of normal adult personality types based on three innate libidinal drives and how they developed in early years. He named them Erotic, Narcissistic, and Compulsive. He further explained that these drives rarely resulted in pure types in adults, and that blends of any two and an even mixture of all three could develop and be observed. This led him to describe seven normal personality types. In that article, he stated: "It is clear that the variety of individual human beings making up the general picture of mankind is almost infinite. Whoever undertakes the justifiable task of differentiating separate types within this multitude, from the beginning is free to select the distinguishing characteristics and princples which shall determine this classification" (Freud, 1932, p. 3).

### Jung's Typology

Carl Jung, who had split from Freud by the time the above-referenced article was written, *did* select different characteristics for his classification. Jung (1923) did not include Freud's descriptions of drives as a basis for his typology; instead, he used mental processes or functions and attitudes, which he believed were innate. Jung specifically identified eight types, beginning with a difference between the attitudes of introversion and extraversion. He claimed that introversion or extraversion, paired with one of four cognitive functions, could describe significant personality differences, depending on which of the four cognitive functions (thinking, feeling, sensing, or intuition) was dominant for each person.

### Modification of Freud's and Jung's Typologies

Freud's and Jung's typologies were subsequently modified by others. The most well-known modification of Jung's work is the MBTI (Myers-Briggs Type

Indicator), which made explicit the inferred dichotomy of judging and perceiving and increased the number of types from eight to 16 (Briggs Myers, McCaulley, Quenk, & Hammer, 1998).

While Freud's psychoanalytic ideas gave rise to a movement, his character typology inspired less ongoing work. However, Erich Fromm (1947) advanced Freud's early typology; he described three non-productive orientations (receptive, exploitative, and hoarding) that were similar to Freud's and added a fourth, the marketing orientation. For Fromm, personality is "the totality of inherited and acquired psychic qualities which are characteristic of one individual and which make one individual unique" (1947, p. 50). Fromm was also concerned with an ideal type, which he referred to as the productive orientation. Fromm's colleague, Michael Maccoby, subsequently modified Fromm's work; he described 16 personality types in a leadership context. The types were based on the four primary types and combinations of primary and secondary types (Maccoby, 2007; Maccoby & Scudder, 2010).

Elias Porter, who split from Carl Rogers over the ethical use of personality tests (Gordon, 1998), used Fromm's four types as the basis for several assessments. Near the end of his career, Porter (1976) stopped attempting to directly measure Fromm's marketing orientation and instead directly measured only the other three in the Strength Deployment Inventory. After a series of different typologies, Porter arrived at a set of seven personality types, based on three primary drives. Porter found that the personalities of people whose scores on the scales for these three primary motivations were fairly close together were similar to what Fromm described as the marketing orientation. Porter's seven Motivational Value System (MVS) types align conceptually with Freud's (1932) seven types and are a "re-discovery" of these types; neither Porter nor Fromm ever referenced this late and little-known work of Freud.

**Traits and Factors vs. Systems of Drives and Motives**

The terms drives and motives, while often used interchangeably, are different. Drives tend to be more innate and less conscious than motives. Motives are pressure or energy toward action; they tend to be more learned and more conscious and purposive than drives are. Traits are characteristics that produce routine behavior, which is not necessarily motivated (Maddi, 1996). However, there is a debate about whether personality factors, such as extraversion, create multiple, discrete traits or whether traits combine to form factors (Wilt, Condon, Brown-Riddell, & Revelle, 2012).

Traits may also be confused with values. The same word may sometimes describe a trait and at other times describe a value. For example, fairness may be a trait if a person generally behaves without bias; fairness may be a value if fairness motivates (or gives energy and purpose to) a person's behavior (Parks & Guay, 2009). The interaction of traits and motives may also explain behavior in different contexts. For example, a person who is a risk taker may drive cautiously when children are in the car if he or she is motivated to protect the children.

## The Driven Personality

What drives are part of personality? Freud (1905/1961, 1930/1961) identified sexual and aggressive drives. His earliest personality types resulted from the assumed fixation of energy in different stages of development.

Fromm (1947) focused primarily on the drive for relatedness, to one's environment, to other people, and to oneself. Fromm's personality types result from the different, non-productive forms of relatedness: receptive, exploitative, hoarding, and marketing.

Maccoby's (1995) concept of drives is more dynamic, with a set of psychic drives that are assumed to be innate: survival, information, mastery, play, relatedness, dignity, and meaning. For Maccoby, the drives combine in different ways to form different personality types, the behavioral characteristics of which are similar to Fromm's and Freud's.

For Porter (1976), the universal drives are for relatedness and feelings of self-worth (akin to dignity in Maccoby's system). Porter's personality types describe different ways of achieving feelings of self-worth in relationships with others. Porter proposed a dual-state view of personality. A set of seven types describes personality in the "going well" state, and a set of 13 types describes the state of conflict. As previously noted, the seven "going well" types were based on Fromm's work and have a strong conceptual connection to Freud's seven libidinal types. The conflict types, however, do not have a conceptual forebear and are Porter's original concept.

The above referenced theoreticians made psychological drives an important part of their typologies. They suggest that types can be understood and explained, at least in part, by the way these drives are shaped during socialization. Jung, however, did not believe that drives had much influence on behavior (Maddi, 1996). Instead, he suggested that the focus of energy and mental processes could explain behavior. To risk oversimplification for the sake of clarity: Drive theorists would suggest that drives and motives give rise to decisions and actions; adherents to Jung's theory would suggest that drives and motives are the result of inherited mental processes. Either way, drives and cognitive processes are related.

**The SDI View of Personality Types**

In the SDI, personality types are described as dynamic systems of motivations that are expressed differently in different conditions. Porter (1976) claimed that affective states interact with motivation to produce qualitatively different behaviors under two perceived conditions, 1) things going well and 2) conflict situations. The SDI is a dual-state personality assessment; it offers two sets of types for two affective states. Each person has one of seven Motivational Value System types and one of thirteen Conflict Sequence types, which yield 91 combinations. Relationship Awareness Theory acknowledges that even these types are not sufficient to describe everything about people. Porter suggested that a full consideration of personality should account for people's concept formation, especially the self-concept. His early work in clinical and therapeutic settings enabled him to observe changes in behavior that followed changes in people's self-concept (Porter, 1950, 1976; Rogers, 1951).

Some of Porter's work with Rogers involved the use of Q-methodology, a technique developed by Stephenson (1935) that Porter applied to the *Portrait of Personal Strengths*. In Q-sorts, the significance of personality traits is based on how those traits interact with other traits (Stephenson, 1950). People of the same personality type may have different traits, or their similar traits may have different meanings.

Relationship Awareness Theory does account for and explain behavior, but behavior is not the basis for personality types. Rather, the basis for types is motivation or purposive strivings. The SDI's personality types are based on why people do things; the focus is on the motive for behavior, not on the behavior itself.

One of the factors that distinguishes people from other animals is intentionality (Rosenberg, 2008); therefore, a personality typology that focuses on motivations, rather than behavior, is a uniquely human typology. The SDI describes personality types, which have their origins in enduring motivations, and the *Portrait of Personal Strengths* (a Q-sort) engages people in an exploration of the way they use their strengths and what their strengths mean to them.

## Is Personality the Result of Nature or Nurture?

Were people born with their Motivational Value Systems and Conflict Sequences, or are these the result of childhood experiences?

The nature-nurture debate is based on a false dichotomy. The tabla rasa (blank slate) assumption of human potential is simply wrong (Funder, 2001), as is pure genetic determinism. People are not blank slates upon which society and the environment can write anything, nor is DNA destiny. From an evolutionary perspective, genetics and the environment are closely intertwined. "The only pertinent questions therefore are (1) which of the various genetic potentialities will be actualized as a consequence of a particular series of life-events in a given physical, social, and cultural environment? and (2) what limits to the development of this personality are set by genetic constitution?" (Kluckhohn & Murray, 1948, p. 38)

Humans have fewer genetic instincts than other animals. We are not hardwired for specific behaviors. However, our genetic code appears to include epigenetic rules (Wilson, 2012). Epigenetic rules are predispositions for learning, phobias, attractions, language, and more that are based on many thousands or millions of years of evolution. The environment that people find themselves in may influence which of these genes are activated and how. But these rules are not beyond conscious control and therefore cannot be considered instincts.

Socialization can instill deep values in people, and people who are socialized in different ways can have different values. Erich Fromm (1947) described the results of these processes as social character. Social character is the set of values and attitudes shared by most people in a society. Fromm, who believed in the perfectibility of human nature (but within its genetic limits), described non-productive personality types as variations on the social character. His productive orientation was based on the ideal of loving productivity, which he believed could contribute to a better society (Fromm, 1955). For Fromm, the study of personality was a tool to critique the way society shaped people and to recommend ways to improve society and the productive development of people in society.

## The SDI View of the Nature-Nurture Debate

Porter was deeply influenced by Fromm's writing while he was working closely with Carl Rogers at the University of Chicago's Counseling Center. In retrospect, this put him squarely in the center of a philosophical debate about human nature. Fromm and Rogers shared an interest in productive human development, but Fromm's vision of human perfectibility was different from Rogers' vision of human potential. Fromm argued that all people could develop toward an ideal, while Rogers (1961) argued that people should develop their individual potential.

Porter did not address the issue of innate vs. socialized personality types in his written work. However, in videotaped training programs, he expressed his opinion that at least some portion of the Motivational Value System was inborn. He cited his experience working with nurses, who could tell differences in personalities in newborn infants (Porter, c. 1980). Given Porter's academic and clinical experience and the views of those who influenced him, such as Fromm, Rogers, Kluckhohn, and Murray, it is reasonable to claim that the SDI view of personality is dialectical; it is a result of the interaction of nature and nurture.

The SDI concept of personality is consistent with Michael Maccoby's (2010), which claims that innate drives become values as people are socialized and that these values become part of people's identities.

The ego in Maccoby's model is the same conscious, reasoning facility as Freud's (1923/1961). The social character is the same as Fromm's (1947) concept of shared values and attitudes.

In some ways—like Fromm's intent to improve society—the SDI explores personality with the implied promise of improving relationships and increasing productiveness. In some ways, like Rogers' intent to value and nurture the individual, the SDI is intended to increase self-awareness and contribute to the development of more congruent functioning.

## Is the Person or the Situation Responsible for Behavior?

There is a *Far Side* cartoon by Gary Larson titled "The four basic personality types." In it, four different people approach the same table that has a glass of water on it. The first says, "The glass is half full!" The second says, "The glass is half empty." The third says, "Half full... No! Wait! Half empty!.. No, half... what was the question?" The fourth says, "Hey! I ordered a cheeseburger!"

Larson has, perhaps unintentionally, provided a useful illustration of Kurt Lewin's famous equation: B=f(P,E). Behavior is a function of an interaction between a person and that person's environment (Lewin, 1998). In Larson's cartoon, the environment is the same for each person, and the behavior of each person is clearly different. The reader is left, then, to deduce the personalities of the four cartoon characters, which might be that they are, respectively, 1) optimistic, 2) pessimistic, 3) indecisive, and 4) demanding. Readers may find humor in the cartoon if they conclude that they could sort people they know into the four categories.

Lewin's equation suggests that behavior is a function of the person and the environment. However, some researchers and theorists have operated under the assumption that there are no meaningful differences among people; therefore, descriptions of personality types could serve no useful purpose (Weiner & Greene, 2008). If the person is removed from the equation or held constant, the environment alone can be used to predict and control behavior. The quest to explain behavior based on the environment led to schools of thought including radical behaviorism or the pairing of stimulus and response, social learning theory and the focus on changing the environment in order to affect a change in behavior, and interactionism and the idea that role expectancies shape behavior (Barnouw, 1985; Goldhaber, 2000; Maddi, 1996).

The popularity of these mechanistic approaches led to a decrease in the perceived value of personality theory. Carl Rogers (1961) attacked mechanistic approaches, such as those advocated by B. F. Skinner. But he and other humanists also questioned the morality of personality assessment on the basis that personality tests were prejudicial and offered limited categories; they claimed that a person could only be understood as a unique individual (Weiner & Greene, 2008). These humanists minimized the role of the environment in Lewin's equation; they claimed that behavior was primarily a function of the person.

The interaction of a trait and an environment may produce a certain behavior, but this idea is incomplete. More complex models of behavior attempt to explain behavior as the dynamic interaction of cognition, affect, and motivation in a given situation (Kammrath, Mendoza-Denton, & Mischel, 2005). Other models include behavior in the mix, rather than viewing behavior as an output of a system. The ABCD model integrates these elements. Affect includes moods, emotions, and preferences. Behavior is motor activity such as walking and talking. Cognition is the process of making meaning, modes of thinking, and problem solving. Desires are motivations or strivings (Wilt, Oehlberg, & Revelle, 2011). When behavior is viewed as part of a human system, rather than just an output, more complex explanations are possible. For example, a valued behavior can improve a person's affective state, and this improved mood can contribute to another valued behavior.

The person-situation debate has been declared over; the winner is both, and the loser is neither. The end of the debate has been signaled by two key recognitions in academic literature: 1) Behavior of individuals correlates between situations, and 2) the person-situation debate was based on a false dichotomy (Funder, 2001). More recently, even those who were strong proponents of the situational approach, such as Walter Mischel, have joined the integrative conversation, writing: "Over the past decade, however, this long-standing person–situation dichotomy has been challenged by a notable development in the personality literature that is just beginning to impact research and thinking in person perception. Namely, it has been discovered that interactive effects between dispositions and situations are common, everyday expressions of personality" (Kammrath, et al., 2005, pp. 198-199).

## The SDI View of the Person and Situation

The SDI's contribution to the person-situation conversation is to split situations into two kinds: 1) situations when people feel good about themselves and 2) situations when people experience conflict. The natures of situations are determined by the perceptions of the people in the situations, not by any outside, objective criteria.

When things are going well, the same motives may underlie different behaviors in different situations. Relationship Awareness Theory (Porter, 1996) describes three intentional styles of relating to others: 1) the Valued Relating Style, which is characterized by a person feeling free to choose behavior, 2) the Borrowed Relating Style, which is characterized by a conscious choice to use non-preferred behavior in pursuit of desired outcomes, and 3) the Mask Relating Style, which is characterized by the use of non-preferred behaviors in an effort to avoid negative consequences. The SDI view of behaviorism and manipulating an environment to produce desired actions, is that these efforts sometimes succeed at producing desired actions. However, when they succeed, it may be at the expense of forcing people into a Mask Relating Style, which is incongruent, stressful, and not sustainable.

Similarly, in conflict situations, motives may underlie different behaviors in different conflicts. While the Conflict Sequence describes changes in motivation and behavior during conflict, there may be variability within each stage. Just as people can borrow or mask behavior when things are going well, they can borrow or mask behavior during conflict.

Porter was also heavily influenced by Lewin's theory. Although Lewin expressed the equation $B=f(P,E)$, it was not intended to be subject to the rules of algebra (as the radical behaviorists attempted). The person interacting with the environment is a complex situation that must account for the whole person, for their motives, values, beliefs, feelings, cognitive processes, and perceptions. This is also the SDI view. Relationship Awareness Theory, though, makes it clear that the environment in which people interact includes other people; one person's behavior is part of the environment that another person perceives.

## DOES PERSONALITY CHANGE?

Do people's Motivational Value Systems and Conflict Sequences change over time, or do they remain the same for their whole life?

Some theorists (Fromm, 1947; Kluckhohn & Murray, 1948; Maddi, 1996) define personality as the unchanging psychological qualities of persons. But these definitions are generally meant to describe adults, and these theorists also talk about development. If personality develops at least in part through socialization, there must be some changes during this development, especially in youth. Developmental stage theorists, such as Erikson (1963), suggest a series of existential conflicts that must be resolved as a person grows and develops.

But does personality change in adulthood? One study of young adults in college found positive changes over a period of two-and-a-half years; participants in this study became more open, more conscientious, and less neurotic as measured by a five-factor assessment (Vaidya, Gray, Haig, & Watson, 2002). The researchers attributed part of this observed change in personality assessment results to a change in the environment; many students were free from parental control for the first time in their lives, and their environment required more self-direction. Stability in personality gradually increases until about age 30, after which personality factors remain relatively stable (Terracciano, McCrae, & Costa Jr., 2010). Other research indicates that values shaped during socialization change more in youth than in adulthood (Parks & Guay, 2009), and findings from research on twins suggest a strong genetic foundation for stability of personality factors in adulthood (Johnson, McGue, & Krueger, 2005).

Personality does appear to change as it develops, but the rate of change appears to slow in adulthood, though some change is still possible. Different adults' rates of change seem to plateau at different levels. One possible explanation for this is that people who score high on openness to experience are more likely to change, as are people with a high degree of neuroticism, which has been linked to depression and other changes (Parks & Guay, 2009).

People may report that significant life experiences triggered a change in personality. However, in one telling study of adults who emigrated to the United States to escape persecution in Nazi Germany, the underlying characteristics of personality were found to remain essentially unchanged, despite the traumatic experiences (Allport, Bruner, & Jandorf, 1948). The researchers did describe changes in behaviors during the transition, but these were explained as temporary responses to the environment, rather than changes in personality. They were interpreted as changes in the way personality manifested itself in different situations.

Philosophically, the question of whether personality changes in adulthood can also raise questions of self-awareness. People who experience significant life changes may believe that their personality has changed as a result of these experiences. However, the possibility exists that the new environment simply was conducive to personality factors those people had previously repressed. Alternatively, a new situation may activate a predisposition that was always part of their potential. Hence, people's experience of change may, upon further analysis, actually represent an act of self-discovery or the development of an undeveloped part of their personalities.

Some theorists, such as Robert Kegan (1994), claim that development is characterized by progressive levels of consciousness. Kegan's subject-object theory holds that whatever is subject at one level of consciousness becomes the object at the next level. Therefore, as adults develop, they experience their self-concepts subjectively at first. They are who they are. Then at the next stage of development, they are able to intentionally alter their self-concepts, to engage in self-authorship. At a higher level of development, people are able to act *on* their self-concepts, instead of being limited to acting *from* their self-concepts.

Personality is not necessarily a result, nor is it a permanently fixed entity. Murray and Kluckhohn (1948) describe personality as process, a dynamic and systemic concept that requires the understanding of the whole person as a prerequisite for explaining the parts of any person. Their concept of a whole personality suggests the integration of multiple drives at any given moment, as well as the consistent integration of drives during a long period of development. Development is characterized by the resolution of major life dilemmas. For them, "the chief over-all function of personality, then, is to create a design for living which permits the periodic and harmonious appeasement of most of its needs as well as gradual progressions towards distant goals. At the highest level of integration, a design of this sort is equivalent to a philosophy of life" (Murray & Kluckhohn, 1948, p. 32).

## The SDI View of Changes in Personality

Theoretically, the SDI is aligned with the idea that personality is relatively stable and unchanging in adults. However, this position is also compatible with the concept of continued adult development. Whether development is thought of as resolving existential conflicts (Erikson, 1963), moving through levels of consciousness (Kegan, 1994), becoming self-actualized (Maslow, 1954; Rogers, 1961), or the productive unfolding of one's powers (Fromm, 1947), the motivational or purposive aspects of personality are viewed as relatively stable, but they are expressed differently as people develop. This is consistent with Porter's (1976) view that behavior changes follow changes in self-concept. Changes in self-concept, however, do not require a change in the underlying motivational structure of personality.

Practically, the SDI measures personality, and people are often curious about whether their SDI results will change. SDI scores are reliable within +/- six points (Porter, 1996), and the results for most people are fairly consistent over time. However, significant changes in SDI results can be observed. Generally, these changes fall into two categories:

1. Mindset: If the SDI is completed correctly (with a whole-life focus) on one occasion, then compared to an incorrectly completed SDI—for example, about a specific role or relationship on another occasion—there are likely to be differences in the results of the two

SDIs. However, these differences do not represent a change in personality. Rather, they represent different expressions of personality in different situations.

2. Mask: In some cases, the SDI may be completed with the intent of using a whole-life focus, but people's responses may be influenced by situations in which they are consciously or unconsciously using mask behavior. If on a later occasion people are free from the mask, differences in SDI results are to be expected. This does not indicate that people's personalities have changed. Rather, their awareness of their personalities has changed—or their willingness to respond honestly to the SDI items has changed. People who are using Mask Relating Styles may have self-concepts that include compliance with external demands, but when free from the masks, their self-concepts could include awareness of their true motivations. People who have experiences of this nature may claim that their personalities have changed, and for them, those are valid experiences. However, further reflection may lead them to conclude that they shed false self-concepts and discovered truer self-concepts that were previously hidden behind the masks.

In summary, the SDI view of changes in personality is that it changes very little in adulthood. However, people continue to develop and are able to become more effective.

## CONCLUSION

The questions posed at the beginning of this chapter were: 1) What are personality types? 2) Is personality the result of nature or nurture? 3) Is the person or the situation responsible for behavior? and 4) Does personality change?

While these questions may continue to generate debate and research, their answers, from an SDI point of view may be simply stated here, on the other side of complexity.

1. What are personality types? Personality is a dynamic system of motivations that are experienced under two conditions: when things are going well and when there is conflict. Types based on a purposive view of personality have great explanatory power; they help people to understand their own behavior and the behavior of others and to make more informed choices about behavior in relationships.

2. Is personality the result of nature or nurture? Personality is the result of both nature and nurture. Innate potential is developed in different ways in different contexts; the debate between nature and nurture represents and always has represented a false choice.

3. Is the person or the situation responsible for behavior? Behavior, as Kurt Lewin originally stated, is a function of the person interacting with that person's environment. Because people have emotions, drives, consciousness, and purposes, understanding behavior requires an understanding of whole persons in their environment.

4. Does personality change? Personality remains relatively stable in adulthood. However, people can develop without changing the motivational structure of their personality. They can become more aware of their personality and more effective at expressing it in their relationships.

*"In the art of living, we are both the artist and the object of our art; we are the sculptor and the marble; the physician and the patient"*
— Erich Fromm, 1947, p. 18

## REFERENCES

Allport, G. W., Bruner, J. S., & Jandorf, E. M. (1948). Personality Under Social Catastrophe. In C. Kluckhohn & H. A. Murray (Eds.), *Personality in Nature, Society, and Culture* (pp. 347-366). New York, NY: Alfred A Knopf.

Barnouw, V. (1985). *Culture and Personality* (Fourth ed.). Belmont, CA: Wadsworth Publishing Company.

Briggs Myers, I., McCaulley, M. H., Quenk, N. L., & Hammer, A. L. (1998). *MBTI Manual*. Palo Alto, CA: Consulting Psychologists Press.

Erikson, E. H. (1963). *Childhood and Society* (Second ed.). New York, NY: W.W. Norton & Company.

Freud, S. (1905/1961). Three Essays on the Theory of Sexuality. In J. Strachey (Ed.), *The Standard Edition of the Complete Psychological Works of Sigmund Freud* (Vol. VII (1901-5), pp. 125-243). London: Hogarth Press.

Freud, S. (1923/1961). The Ego and the Id. In J. Strachey (Ed.), *The Standard Edition of the Complete Psychological Works of Sigmund Freud* (Vol. XIX (1923-25)). London: Hogarth Press.

Freud, S. (1930/1961). Civilization and its Discontents. In J. Strachey (Ed.), *The Standard Edition of the Complete Psychological Works of Sigmund Freud* (Vol. XXI (1927-31), pp. 59-145). London: Hogarth Press.

Freud, S. (1932). Libidinal Types. *Psychoanalytic Quarterly,* 1(1), 3-6.

Fromm, E. (1947). *Man for Himself: An inquiry into the psychology of ethics.* New York, NY: Henry Holt and Company.

Fromm, E. (1955). *The Sane Society.* New York, NY: Henry Holt and Company.

Funder, D. C. (2001). Personality. *Annual Review of Psychology,* 52, 197-221.

Goldhaber, D. E. (2000). *Theories of Human Development: Integrative perpsectives.* Mountain View, CA: Mayfield Publishing Company.

Gordon, T. (1998). [Interview conducted by Tim Scudder].

Johnson, W., McGue, M., & Krueger, R. F. (2005). Personality Stability in Late Adulthood: A behavioral genetic analysis. *Journal of Personality,* 73(2), 523-552.

Jung, C. G. (1923). *Psychological Types.* New York, NY: Harcourt Brace.

Kammrath, L. K., Mendoza-Denton, R., & Mischel, W. (2005). Incorporating If... Then... Personality Signatures in Person Perception: Beyond the person-situation dichotomy. *Journal of Personality and Social Psychology,* 88(4), 605-618.

Kegan, R. (1994). *In Over Our Heads: The mental demands of modern life.* Cambridge, MA: Harvard University Press.

Kluckhohn, C., & Murray, H. A. (1948). Personality Formation: The determinants. In C. Kluckhohn & H. A. Murray (Eds.), *Personality in Nature, Society, and Culture* (pp. 35-48). New York, NY: Alfred A Knopf.

Lewin, M. A. (1998). Kurt Lewin: His psychology and a daughter's recollections. In G. A. Kimble & M. Wertheimer (Eds.), *Portraits of Pioneers in Psychology* (Vol. III, pp. 105-118). Washington, DC: American Psychological Association.

Maccoby, M. (1995). *Why Work?* (2nd ed.). Alexandria, VA: Miles River Press.

Maccoby, M. (2007). *Narcissistic Leaders*. Boston, MA: Harvard Business School Press.

Maccoby, M., & Scudder, T. (2010). *Becoming a Leader We Need with Strategic Intelligence*. Carlsbad, CA: Personal Strengths Publishing.

Maddi, S. R. (1996). *Personality Theories* (Sixth ed.). Long Grove, IL: Waveland Press.

Maslow, A. H. (1954). *Motivation and Personality*. New York, NY: Harper & Brothers.

McCrae, R. R. (2011). Personality Theories for the 21st Century. *Teaching of Psychology*, 38(3), 209-214.

Murray, H. A., & Kluckhohn, C. (1948). Outline of a Conception of Personality. In C. Kluckhohn & H. A. Murray (Eds.), *Personality in Nature, Society, and Culture* (pp. 3-32). New York, NY: Alfred A Knopf.

Parks, L., & Guay, R. P. (2009). Personality, Values, and Motivation. *Personality and Individual Differences*, 47, 675-684.

Porter, E. H. (1950). *Introduction to Therapeutic Counseling*. Cambridge, MA: The Riverside Press.

Porter, E. H. (1976). On the Development of Relationship Awareness Theory: A personal note. *Group & Organization Management*, 1(3), 302-309.

Porter, E. H. (1996). *Relationship Awareness Theory*. Carlsbad, CA: Personal Strengths Publishing.

Porter, E. H. (c. 1980). Archival Video. Carlsbad, CA: Personal Strengths Publishing.

Rogers, C. R. (1951). *Client Centered Therapy*. Boston: Houghton Mifflin.

Rogers, C. R. (1961). *On Becoming a Person*. New York, NY: Houghton Mifflin Company.

Rosenberg, A. (2008). *Philosophy of Social Science* (3rd ed.). Boulder, CO: Westview Press.

Stephenson, W. (1935). Correlating Persons Instead of Tests. *Character and Personality*, 4, 17-24.

Stephenson, W. (1950). The Significance of Q-technique for the Study of Personality. In M. L. Reymert (Ed.), *Feelings and Emotions: The mooseheart symposium* (pp. 552-570). New York, NY: McGraw-Hill.

Terracciano, A., McCrae, R. R., & Costa Jr., P. T. (2010). Intra-Individual Change in Personality Stability and Age. *Journal of Research in Personality*, 44, 31-37.

Vaidya, J. G., Gray, E. K., Haig, J., & Watson, D. (2002). On the Temporal Stability of Personality: Evidence for differential stability and the role of life experiences. *Journal of Personality and Social Psychology*, 83(6), 1469-1484.

Weiner, I. B., & Greene, R. L. (2008). *Handbook of Personality Assessment*. Hoboken, NJ: Wiley.

Wilson, E. O. (2012). *The Social Conquest of Earth*. New York, NY: Liveright Publishing Corporation.

Wilt, J., Condon, D. M., Brown-Riddell, A., & Revelle, W. (2012). Fundamental Questions in Personality. *European Journal of Personality*, 26, 629-631.

Wilt, J., Oehlberg, K., & Revelle, W. (2011). Anxiety in Personality. *Personality and Individual Differences*, 50(7), 987-993.

# Frequency of SDI Types

The following tables report numerical and percentage frequencies of the seven Motivational Value Systems, the 13 Conflict Sequences, and the 91 (7x13) possible combinations of MVS and CS. These data were randomly selected from the OnlineSDI database. They reflect the SDI results of people who recently completed the SDI online in English in the United States. Demographic data were not collected, but given that most SDIs are used in training and development efforts within organizations, it is safe to assume that the data represent a population predominantly comprised of working adults who reside in the United States.

No special significance should be attached to the zeros in the table; a different sample might yield zeros where there are currently ones or twos, and vice-versa. However, the sample size is large enough to consider some generalizations for the US population. For examples, people with a Red-Green MVS rarely have Blue as their first stage of conflict, people with a Green MVS rarely have Green as their third stage of conflict, and people with a Blue MVS are most likely to have Red as their third stage of conflict.

**Figure 4.2** *Cross-tabulation of MVS and CS Types: Counts*

|  | Blue | Red | Green | Red-Blue | Red-Green | Blue-Green | Hub | Total |
|---|---|---|---|---|---|---|---|---|
| B-R-G | 20 | 3 | 1 | 16 | 0 | 3 | 6 | 49 |
| B-G-R | 332 | 11 | 17 | 92 | 1 | 120 | 82 | 655 |
| B-(RG) | 91 | 6 | 1 | 53 | 2 | 25 | 41 | 219 |
| R-B-G | 10 | 16 | 1 | 18 | 1 | 0 | 10 | 56 |
| R-G-B | 24 | 152 | 28 | 56 | 51 | 16 | 114 | 441 |
| R-(BG) | 21 | 59 | 5 | 58 | 9 | 6 | 51 | 209 |
| G-B-R | 325 | 56 | 130 | 132 | 16 | 278 | 361 | 1,298 |
| G-R-B | 66 | 128 | 135 | 77 | 73 | 73 | 247 | 799 |
| G-(BR) | 157 | 70 | 137 | 120 | 42 | 135 | 410 | 1,071 |
| (BR)-G | 24 | 6 | 1 | 43 | 0 | 3 | 12 | 89 |
| (RG)-B | 34 | 127 | 42 | 87 | 53 | 31 | 178 | 552 |
| (BG)-R | 272 | 28 | 36 | 98 | 8 | 142 | 222 | 806 |
| (BRG) | 116 | 83 | 24 | 157 | 6 | 52 | 318 | 756 |
| Total | 1,492 | 745 | 558 | 1,007 | 262 | 884 | 2,052 | 7,000 |

**Figure 4.3** *Cross-tabulation of MVS and CS Types: Percentages*

|  | Blue | Red | Green | Red-Blue | Red-Green | Blue-Green | Hub | Total |
|---|---|---|---|---|---|---|---|---|
| B-R-G | 0.29% | 0.04% | 0.01% | 0.23% | 0.00% | 0.04% | 0.09% | 0.70% |
| B-G-R | 4.74% | 0.16% | 0.24% | 1.31% | 0.01% | 1.71% | 1.17% | 9.36% |
| B-(RG) | 1.30% | 0.09% | 0.01% | 0.76% | 0.03% | 0.36% | 0.59% | 3.13% |
| R-B-G | 0.14% | 0.23% | 0.01% | 0.26% | 0.01% | 0.00% | 0.14% | 0.80% |
| R-G-B | 0.34% | 2.17% | 0.40% | 0.80% | 0.73% | 0.23% | 1.63% | 6.30% |
| R-(BG) | 0.30% | 0.84% | 0.07% | 0.83% | 0.13% | 0.09% | 0.73% | 2.99% |
| G-B-R | 4.64% | 0.80% | 1.86% | 1.89% | 0.23% | 3.97% | 5.16% | 18.54% |
| G-R-B | 0.94% | 1.83% | 1.93% | 1.10% | 1.04% | 1.04% | 3.53% | 11.41% |
| G-(BR) | 2.24% | 1.00% | 1.96% | 1.71% | 0.60% | 1.93% | 5.86% | 15.30% |
| (BR)-G | 0.34% | 0.09% | 0.01% | 0.61% | 0.00% | 0.04% | 0.17% | 1.27% |
| (RG)-B | 0.49% | 1.81% | 0.60% | 1.24% | 0.76% | 0.44% | 2.54% | 7.89% |
| (BG)-R | 3.89% | 0.40% | 0.51% | 1.40% | 0.11% | 2.03% | 3.17% | 11.51% |
| (BRG) | 1.66% | 1.19% | 0.34% | 2.24% | 0.09% | 0.74% | 4.54% | 10.80% |
| **Total** | 21.31% | 10.64% | 7.97% | 14.39% | 3.74% | 12.63% | 29.31% | 100.00% |

N=7,000

# Notes

## Part 1: Introduction

1. Like all languages, the language of Relationship Awareness Theory and the SDI has evolved over the years. Readers who are familiar with earlier works will notice subtle changes for clarity and utility, and the addition of terms and concepts that align Relationship Awareness Theory with current trends in theory and practice.

2. Definitions of the ten terms shown in the iceberg model were derived from several sources. *New Oxford American Dictionary*, Third ed., (New York: Oxford University Press, 2010); Laura Parks and Russell P. Guay, "Personality, Values, and Motivation," *Personality and Individual Differences* 47 (2009); Salvatore R. Maddi, *Personality Theories*, Sixth ed., (Long Grove, IL: Waveland Press, 1996); Elias H. Porter, *Relationship Awareness Theory*, (Carlsbad, CA: Personal Strengths Publishing, 1996); Tim Scudder, ed., *Strength Deployment Inventory Facilitation Guide*, Fourth ed., (Carlsbad, CA: Personal Strengths Publishing, 2009).

3. Porter credited Erich Fromm with the concept of positive and negative aspects of the same traits for people of different personality types. While Fromm critiqued the non-productive orientations, Porter reframed this concept to begin with strengths. Erich Fromm, *Man for Himself: An Inquiry into the Psychology of Ethics*, (New York: Henry Holt and Company, 1947); Elias H. Porter, "On the Development of Relationship Awareness Theory: A Personal Note," *Group & Organization Management* 1, no. 3 (1976), 306.

4. The attributes of frequency, duration, intensity, and context are often used in training and developmental efforts to describe the manner in which strengths are overdone. This is typically linked to the use of the *Portrait of Overdone Strengths*, a Q-sort. For the earliest known reference to this schema with Q-sorts see Norman H. Livson and Thomas F. Nichols, "Discrimination and Reliability in Q-Sort Personality Descriptions," *The Journal of Abnormal and Social Psychology* 52, no. 2 (1957), 159.

5. (see part 1, n. 2).

6. These terms are all unique to Relationship Awareness Theory. Porter introduced the terms Valued Relating Style, Borrowed Relating Style, and Mask Relating Style. The terms Motivational Value System and

Conflict Sequence were not used by Porter, but were introduced after his death (in 1987) to identify concepts he described. Porter, *Relationship Awareness Theory*, 17.

7. Conflict has a specific meaning in Relationship Awareness Theory, as do the terms related to conflict. The terms presented in this section build on Porter's concept and are consistent with those used in recent works about conflict. Porter "On the Development"; Tim Scudder and Michael Patterson, *Have a Nice Conflict Participant Workbook,* (Carlsbad, CA: Personal Strengths Publishing, 2011); Tim Scudder, Michael Patterson, and Kent Mitchell, *Have a Nice Conflict,* (Jossey Bass: San Francisco, CA, 2012). Other definitions of conflict are similar to Relationship Awareness Theory's definition of opposition; for examples see Roger Fisher, William Ury, and Bruce Patton, *Getting to Yes, Negotiating Agreement without Giving In,* Second Edition ed., (New York, NY: Penguin Books, 1991); and Kenneth W. Thomas and Ralph H. Kilmann, "Thomas-Kilmann Conflict Mode Instrument," (Mountain View, CA: Consulting Psychologists Press, 2007).

8. The SDI suite of assessments requires facilitator certification as described at http://www.personalstrengths.com.

9. Porter's dissertation was published in two parts: (1) Elias H. Porter, "The Development and Evaluation of a Measure of Counseling Interview Procedures: Part I the Development," *Educational and Psychological Measurement* 3 (1943); and (2) Elias H. Porter, "The Development and Evaluation of a Measure of Counseling Interview Procedures: Part II the Evaluation," *Educational and Psychological Measurement* 3 (1943); for the dissertation see Elias H. Porter, "The Development and Evaluation of a Measure of Counseling Interview Procedures," (The Ohio State University, 1942).

10. A group of psychologists at the University of Chicago's Counseling Center were trying to help large groups of servicemen who were returning from World War II. They were awarded a contract from the Veterans Administration to help these veterans. They could not train therapists quickly enough to handle the demand, so they organized group conversations, which turned out to be very therapeutic and were the beginning of encounter groups. Rogers specifically mentioned Doug Blocksma, Thomas Gordon, and Elias Porter as members of this team. Carl R. Rogers, Jeffery H.D. Cornelius-White, and Cecily F. Cornelius-White, "Reminiscing and Predicting: Rogers' Beyond Words Speech and Commentary," *Journal of Humanistic Psychology* 45 (1986/2005), 390; Carl R. Rogers, *Client Centered Therapy,* (Boston: Houghton Mifflin, 1951), 444; Irving B. Weiner and Roger L. Greene, *Handbook of Personality Assessment,* (Hoboken, NJ: Wiley, 2008), 7;

for more detail about the program see Doug D. Blocksma and Elias H. Porter, "A Short-Term Training Program in Client-Centered Counseling," *Journal of Consulting Psychology* 11, no. 2 (1947).

11. For examples of Porter's work in experimental psychology see Elias H. Porter, "The Influence of Delayed Instructions to Learn Upon Human Performance," *Journal of Experimental Psychology* 23 (1938); and Elias H. Porter, and Calvin S. Hall, "A Further Investigation of the Role of Emphasis in Learning," *Journal of Experimental Psychology* 22 (1938): 377-83.

12. Howard Kirschenbaum, *On Becoming Carl Rogers,* (New York: Delacorte Press, 1979), 206-7; Carl R. Rogers, *On Becoming a Person,* (New York: Houghton Mifflin Company, 1961), 247.

13. In the forward to Porter's book, Rogers wrote "If I may inject a personal word, I was among the doubters when the author conceived this book. I felt that problems considered on paper could do little to help counselors to recognize and deal with their basic attitudes, and might do real harm by causing them to believe that psychotherapy is a bundle of tricks, a golf bag full of techniques carefully chosen for every purpose, including a niblick to get the unwary counselor out of any sand traps. Consequently, the ingenuity which Dr. Porter has shown in developing devices which compel self-examination and facilitate attitudinal reorganization incites my admiration. He has succeeded where failure seemed almost certain." Elias H. Porter, *Introduction to Therapeutic Counseling,* (Cambridge, MA: The Riverside Press, 1950), viii. Rogers later recommended Porter's work and made several references to it. Rogers, *Client Centered Therapy,* 556.

14. The earliest known example of this was titled the Person-Relatedness Test. Elias H. Porter, "The Person Relatedness Test," (Chicago, IL: Science Research Associates, 1953).

15. Fromm, *Man for Himself.*

16. Thomas Gordon, 1998, Interview with Tim Scudder.

17. Weiner and Greene, *Handbook of Personality Assessment,* 8.

18. Porter, "On the Development," 307.

19. Porter was in partnership with Stuart Atkins and Alan Katcher to market a personality assessment called LIFO. While the three of them shared authorship credit, it was based on Porter's *Person Relatedness Test* and many of the items in the two tests were identical. Prior to working with Atkins and Katcher, Porter had been developing an assessment called

the Strength-Vulnerability Index, the results of which were aligned with Fromm's productive and non-productive orientations, and were renamed in the LIFO assessment. After the breakup of the partnership, Porter founded Personal Strengths Assessment Service, which was later renamed Personal Strengths Publishing, Inc. Stuart Atkins, Allan Katcher, and Elias H. Porter, "LIFO: Life Orientations and Strength Excess Profile," (Los Angeles, CA: Atkins-Katcher Associates, 1967); Fromm, *Man for Himself*; Porter, "Person Relatedness Test"; Elias H. Porter, "Strength-Vulnerability Index (Form B)," (Santa Monica, CA, 1964).

20. Elias Porter credited his wife, Sara Maloney-Porter, DSW, with the idea of using colors to identify the personality types. Elias H. Porter, *Archival Video,* (Carlsbad, CA: Personal Strengths Publishing, c. 1980).

21. This description of character structure was adapted from Fromm, *Man for Himself,* 54-61.

22. "The theory assumes, as does Tolman's theory, that *behavior traits arise from purpose strivings for gratification mediated by concepts or hypotheses as to how to obtain those gratifications.* Put in simplest terms, behavior traits are the consistencies in our behavior that stem from the consistencies in what we find gratifying in interpersonal relationships and the consistencies in our beliefs or concepts as to how to interact with other people in order to achieve those gratifications." Italics in original. Porter, "On the Development," 305-6; Edward C. Tolman, *Purposive Behavior in Animals and Men,* (New York: The Century Company, 1932).

23. For an adaptation of Chris Argyris's Ladder of Inference for use with the SDI see Michael Maccoby, Clifford L. Norman, C. Jane Norman, and Richard Margolies, *Tranforming Health Care Leadership,* (San Francisco: Jossey Bass, in press).

24. For a structured model about creating dialogue that highlights the value of using SDI in conflict dialogue see Peter Nixon, *Dialogue Gap,* (Singapore: John Wiley & Sons, 2012), 258-67.

25. The text in this table is slightly modified from Porter's original statement: "When an individual is free to pursue his gratifications, the nurturant motivation takes the form of actively seeking to be helpful to others, the directive motivation takes the form of self-assertion and seeking opportunities to provide leadership (in the conventional sense of leadership), and the autonomizing motivation takes the form of actively seeking logical orderliness and self-reliance. In the face of conflict and opposition, the nurturant motivation is expressed

in efforts to preserve and restore harmony, the directive motivation is expressed in efforts to prevail over the other person, and the autonomizing motivation is expressed in efforts to conserve resources and assure independence." Porter, "On the Development," 308.

26. Porter, *Relationship Awareness Theory*; Scudder, ed., *Facilitation Guide.*

## PART 2: MOTIVATIONAL VALUE SYSTEMS

1. The test-retest reliability of the SDI is +/- six points. Porter, *Relationship Awareness Theory,* 68.

2. The term congruent is used here with the same meaning as expressed by Carl Rogers. It is the alignment of experience, awareness, and communication. For a full consideration of this concept see "A Tentative Formulation of a General Law of Interpersonal Relationships" in Rogers, *On Becoming a Person,* 338-346.

3. The first SDI, published in 1971, described three types. The first SDI to feature the charting triangle was published in 1973 and identified six types, but provided interpretive text for only three; there was no circle for the Hub in the center. Instead, the boundaries of the other six types continued into the center. Unpublished versions of the triangle showed two different sets of boundaries, each identifying nine types. Early versions of the *Feedback Edition of the SDI* and *Expectations Edition of the SDI* showed as few as six and as many as ten types on the triangle. The fact that Porter finally arrived at a set of seven types is of historical significance, because these seven types are constructed in exactly the same way as the seven normal personality types described in a little-known article by Sigmund Freud, "Libidinal Types," *Psychoanalytic Quarterly* 1, no. 1 (1932): 3-6.

4. Regarding the Hub, Porter said: "We set the boundary more or less empirically at 11 points above and below the mean (33 ⅓) on each side (approximately 1 standard deviation above and below the mean). We have since learned that this may have been too loose since some studies have indicated statistically discriminable differences between inner-hubs (½ SD above and below) and blue-hubs, red-hubs, and green hubs (from ½ SD out to 1 full SD from the mean). At present, however, we see no reason to press for greater precision in what can at best be an arbitrary boundary setting exercise." Porter, *Relationship Awareness Theory,* 67.

5. For a full consideration of learning styles see Sharan B. Merriam, Rosemary S. Cafella, and Lisa M. Baumgartner, *Learning in Adulthood: a Comprehensive Guide,* (San Francisco: Jossey-Bass, 2007).

6.   Five-factor models include Openness to Experience, Conscientious-
     ness, Extraversion, Agreeableness, and Neuroticism. Five-factor theory
     has had a significant affect on personality research and education. For
     a discussion of this see Robert R. McCrae, "Personality Theories for
     the 21st Century," *Teaching of Psychology* 38, no. 3 (2011).

7.   Carl Jung believed that each person had a dominant cognitive func-
     tion, a data collecting function of sensing or intuition, or a decision-
     making function of thinking or feeling. Carl Gustav Jung, *Psychologi-
     cal Types,* (New York: Harcourt Brace, 1923).

8.   The *Portrait of Personal Strengths* is a Q-sort. Q-methodology was in-
     troduced by William Stephenson as a means of analyzing human sub-
     jectivity. Rather than isolating factors and scoring people against these
     factors, users of Q-methodology focus on the whole person, the inter-
     relationships of items, and the meanings these interrelationships have
     for individuals. William Stephenson, "Correlating Persons Instead of
     Tests," *Character and Personality* 4 (1935); William Stephenson, *The
     Study of Behavior: Q-Technique and Its Methodology,* Midway reprint
     ed., (Chicago: The University of Chicago Press, 1953/1975).

## PARTS 2 AND 3: MOTIVATIONAL VALUE SYSTEM AND CONFLICT SEQUENCE DESCRIPTIONS

The descriptions for the Motivational Value Systems and Conflict Sequences
were assembled from many sources. Chief among them were: Porter, "On
the Development"; Porter, *Relationship Awareness Theory*; and Elias H. Porter, "Strength Deployment Inventory," (Carlsbad, CA: Personal Strengths
Publishing, 2005). The authors also referred to descriptions of personality
types in Fromm, *Man for Himself;* and the continued work by Fromm's colleague, Michael Maccoby, *Why Work?* 2nd ed., (Alexandria, VA: Miles River
Press, 1995); Michael Maccoby, *Narcissistic Leaders,* (Boston, MA: Harvard
Business School Press, 2007); Michael Maccoby and Tim Scudder, *Becoming
a Leader We Need with Strategic Intelligence,* (Carlsbad, CA: Personal Strengths
Publishing, 2010); and to Personal Strengths Publishing's archival files and
several out-of-print training resources written by Porter. The authors also drew
from their experience as SDI facilitators, including the work done by learners
during structured training and development programs. The definitions of the
words that make up the Motivational Value System names that are provided at
the beginning of each MVS section were drawn from the *New Oxford American
Dictionary.* In cases where the exact words were not defined in that dictionary,
definitions of similar forms of the words were used to produce the definitions
as provided here.

## Part 3: Conflict Sequences

1. The descriptions of the Conflict Sequences were not included in the SDI until the 1996 edition, which was also the first edition to delineate the Conflict Sequence regions on the triangle, based on Porter's mathematical definitions. Prior to the 1996 SDI, the conflict information was only available in a facilitator's manual and as "Exercise 4" in a workshop kit called the *Basic Course*.

2. (see part 2, n. 1).

3. "As a second major premise, Relationship Awareness Theory holds that there are, at the very least, two clear, distinguishably different conditions in the stimulus world that affect patterns of behavior. One of these conditions exists when we are free to pursue the gratifications we seek from others. The second condition exists when we are faced with conflict and opposition so that we are not free to pursue our gratifications but must resort to the preservation of our own integrity and self-esteem. The behavior traits we exhibit under these two conditions truly differ. When we are free to pursue our gratifications, we are more or less uniformly predictable, but in the face of conflict and opposition we undergo changes in motivations that link into different bodies of beliefs and concepts that are, in turn, expressed in yet different behavior traits. *We are predictably uniform in our behavior when we are free, and we are predictably variable as we meet with obstructing conditions in our stimulus worlds.*" Italics in original. Porter, "On the Development," 306.

4. Porter, *Relationship Awareness Theory*, 25.

5. Table adapted from Tim Scudder and Michael Patterson, *Have a Nice Conflict Participant Workbook,* (Carlsbad, CA: Personal Strengths Publishing, 2011), 57.

# REFERENCES

The following references relate to parts one through three of this book. The chapter "The SDI View of Personality" in part four is presented in American Psychological Association style and includes a separate reference list, which shares some references with those presented here.

Atkins, Stuart, Allan Katcher, and Elias H. Porter. "LIFO: Life Orientations and Strength Excess Profile." Los Angeles, CA: Atkins-Katcher Associates, 1967.

Blocksma, Doug D., and Elias H. Porter. "A Short-Term Training Program in Client-Centered Counseling." *Journal of Consulting Psychology* 11, no. 2 (1947): 55-60.

Fisher, Roger, William Ury, and Bruce Patton. *Getting to Yes, Negotiating Agreement without Giving In.* Second Edition ed. New York, NY: Penguin Books, 1991.

Freud, Sigmund. "Libidinal Types." *Psychoanalytic Quarterly* 1, no. 1 (1932): 3-6.

Fromm, Erich. *Man for Himself: An Inquiry into the Psychology of Ethics.* New York: Henry Holt and Company, 1947.

Gordon, Thomas. 1998, Interview conducted by Tim Scudder.

Jung, Carl Gustav. *Psychological Types.* New York: Harcourt Brace, 1923.

Kirschenbaum, Howard. *On Becoming Carl Rogers.* New York: Delacorte Press, 1979.

Livson, Norman H., and Thomas F. Nichols. "Discrimination and Reliability in Q-Sort Personality Descriptions." *The Journal of Abnormal and Social Psychology* 52, no. 2 (1957): 159-65.

Maccoby, Michael. *Narcissistic Leaders.* Boston: Harvard Business School Press, 2007.

———. *Why Work?* 2nd ed. Alexandria, VA: Miles River Press, 1995.

Maccoby, Michael, Clifford L. Norman, C. Jane Norman, and Richard Margolies. *Tranforming Health Care Leadership.* San Francisco: Jossey Bass, 2013 in press.

Maccoby, Michael, and Tim Scudder. *Becoming a Leader We Need with Strategic Intelligence.* Carlsbad, CA: Personal Strengths Publishing, 2010.

Maddi, Salvatore R. *Personality Theories.* Sixth ed. Long Grove, IL: Waveland Press, 1996.

McCrae, Robert R. "Personality Theories for the 21st Century." *Teaching of Psychology* 38, no. 3 (2011): 209-14.

Merriam, Sharan B., Rosemary S. Cafella, and Lisa M. Baumgartner. *Learning in Adulthood, a Comprehensive Guide.* San Francisco: Jossey-Bass, 2007.

*New Oxford American Dictionary.* Third ed. New York: Oxford University Press, 2010.

Nixon, Peter. *Dialogue Gap.* Singapore: John Wiley & Sons, 2012.

Parks, Laura, and Russell P. Guay. "Personality, Values, and Motivation." *Personality and Individual Differences* 47 (2009): 675-84.

Porter, Elias H. *Archival Video.* Carlsbad, CA: Personal Strengths Publishing, c. 1980.

———. "The Development and Evaluation of a Measure of Counseling Interview Procedures." The Ohio State University, 1942

———. "The Development and Evaluation of a Measure of Counseling Interview Procedures: Part I the Development." *Educational and Psychological Measurement* 3 (1943): 105-26.

———. "The Development and Evaluation of a Measure of Counseling Interview Procedures: Part II the Evaluation." *Educational and Psychological Measurement* 3 (1943): 214-38.

———. "The Influence of Delayed Instructions to Learn Upon Human Performance." *Journal of Experimental Psychology* 23 (1938): 633-40.

———. *Introduction to Therapeutic Counseling.* Cambridge, MA: The Riverside Press, 1950.

———. "On the Development of Relationship Awareness Theory: A Personal Note." *Group & Organization Management* 1, no. 3 (1976): 302-09.

———. "The Person Relatedness Test." Chicago, IL: Science Research Associates, 1953.

———. *Relationship Awareness Theory.* Carlsbad, CA: Personal Strengths Publishing, 1996.

———. "Strength Deployment Inventory." Carlsbad, CA: Personal Strengths Publishing, 2005.

———. "Strength-Vulnerability Index (Form B)." Santa Monica, CA, 1964.

Porter, Elias H., and Calvin S. Hall. "A Further Invesitgation of the Role of Emphasis in Learning." *Journal of Experimental Psychology* 22 (1938): 377-83.

Rogers, Carl R. *Client Centered Therapy.* Boston: Houghton Mifflin, 1951.

———. *On Becoming a Person.* New York: Houghton Mifflin Company, 1961.

Rogers, Carl R., Jeffery H.D. Cornelius-White, and Cecily F. Cornelius-White. "Reminiscing and Predicting: Rogers' Beyond Words Speech and Commentary." *Journal of Humanistic Psychology* 45 (1986/2005).

Scudder, Tim, ed. *Strength Deployment Inventory Facilitation Guide,* Fourth ed. Carlsbad, CA: Personal Strengths Publishing, 2009.

Scudder, Tim, and Michael Patterson. *Have a Nice Conflict Participant Workbook.* Carlsbad, CA: Personal Strengths Publishing, 2011.

Scudder, Tim, Michael Patterson, and Kent Mitchell. *Have a Nice Conflict.* Jossey Bass: San Francisco, 2012.

Stephenson, William. "Correlating Persons Instead of Tests." *Character and Personality* 4 (1935): 17-24.

———. *The Study of Behavior: Q-Technique and Its Methodology.* Midway reprint ed. Chicago: The University of Chicago Press, 1953/1975.

Thomas, Kenneth W., and Ralph H. Kilmann. "Thomas-Kilmann Conflict Mode Instrument." Mountain View, CA: Consulting Psychologists Press, 2007.

Tolman, Edward C. *Purposive Behavior in Animals and Men.* New York: The Century Company, 1932.

Weiner, Irving B., and Roger L. Greene. *Handbook of Personality Assessment.* Hoboken, NJ: Wiley, 2008.

# Acknowledgements

The first and most significant acknowledgement is to Elias Porter, the author of *Relationship Awareness Theory* and the SDI. His work in the 1950s with Carl Rogers at the University of Chicago helped to launch the human potential movement and bring a positive concept of mental health to the growing field of psychology. Porter's ongoing research, development, teaching, and practical application culminated in the founding of Personal Strengths Publishing and the launch of the SDI in 1971.

Porter (who had a Blue MVS and a B-G-R Conflict Sequence) wanted to create a theory that would be *for* people, not *about* people—one that would guide people toward self-discovery. Over 40 years of publication and growth are testament to the enduring power of that philosophy. Without these solid academic foundations, nothing in this book would be possible. Porter's articles, early versions of products, videos, and hand-written notes in the Personal Strengths Publishing archives were an invaluable source for this work.

We would also like to recognize the people who reviewed various drafts or sections of this book and offered suggestions for improvement. Thanks to: Tom Beasor, Gil Brady, Keith Catchpole, Bobby Cross, Kit Davis, Nanette Emrich, Thomas Erdos, Raul Gomez, Donna Hadley, Judy Hemmingsen, Matt Hemmingsen, Ray Linder, Michael Maccoby, Tina Mertel, Kent Mitchell, Prabu Naidu, Annabelle Nelson, Claes Nittzell, Cliff Norman, Chris Osorio, Mike Patterson, Janice Petrucci, Brenda Ratcliff, Lea Symonds, John Thill, Bob Tomkinson, Todd VanDerWerff, and Pam Welsby.

# About the Authors

**Tim Scudder** is the CEO of Personal Strengths Publishing, Inc., an organization that supports transformational learning in relationships in over 20 languages. He is the co-author of *Have a Nice Conflict* and the co-author or editor of several professional development programs including *Becoming a Leader We Need with Strategic Intelligence*, and SDI Certification. He has consulted with the organization development, training, and human resources departments of many corporate, government, military, education, and not-for-profit organizations. He is a Certified Public Accountant and holds a Masters of Arts in Human Development from Fielding Graduate University, where he is completing his doctorate in Human and Organizational Systems.

**Debra LaCroix** has over 20 years of experience as a Master Trainer and Facilitator in diverse settings, ranging from corporate board rooms and city council chambers through manufacturing and service industries to "at-risk" populations and prison classrooms. Her areas of expertise include customized training, keynote presentations, customer service, organizational interventions, leadership development, change management, and comprehensive outplacement. Debra designed and implemented a multi-national Shoreside Leadership Institute for Princess Cruises. She served as the Director of Protocol Administration for the 1984 Los Angeles Olympic Organizing Committee. Her Bachelor's Degree and California Lifetime Teaching Credential are from California Lutheran University. She has completed the coursework for a Master's Degree in Education Administration.

# Index

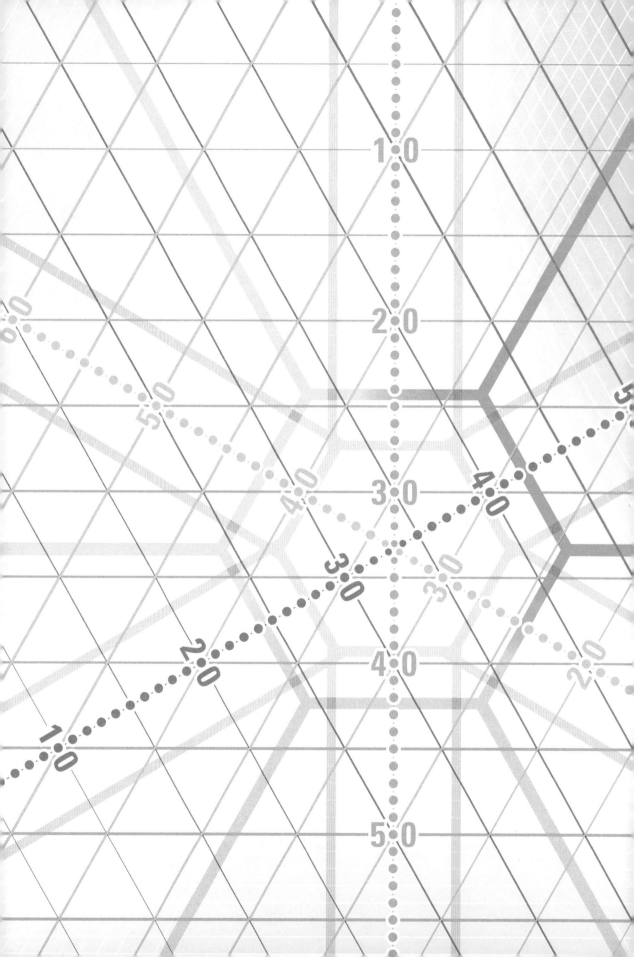

PERSONAL
STRENGTHS
PUBLISHING

Personal Strengths Publishing,® Inc. is the company behind the SDI® (*Strength Deployment Inventory*®) and other inventories based on the theory of Relationship Awareness®—a group of ideas that help provide a window into the motivation that drives behavior.

Founded over forty years ago, PSP is based in Carlsbad, California and serves customers through a global network of interrelated distributors who offer products and services in three main categories:

1. Training and development services: direct training for teams and individuals.

2. Train the trainer services: SDI certification, co-facilitation, and curriculum design.

3. SDI and related products: assessments, workplace learning tools, books, videos, and other paper and electronic resources. The SDI is available in over twenty languages.

SDI assessments are available for use by certified facilitators who successfully complete the SDI Certification training. Facilitators may be independent or employed by any type of organization. As such, training and development services that incorporate the SDI are available from many individual consultants and large consulting organizations. The capacity for delivery of these services can also be developed within an organization's training, human resources, organization development, or other similar departments.

For more information on the SDI and other Relationship Awareness tools or to find your regional distributor, please visit www.PersonalStrengths.com.